The Siege of Charleston

And the operations on the south Atlantic Coast in the war amoung the states

Samuel Jones

Alpha Editions

This edition published in 2019

ISBN : 9789353800833

Design and Setting By
Alpha Editions
email - alphaedis@gmail.com

THE SIEGE OF CHARLESTON

AND THE OPERATIONS ON THE SOUTH ATLANTIC COAST IN THE WAR AMONG THE STATES

BY

SAMUEL JONES

Formerly Major-General C. S. A.

NEW YORK
THE NEALE PUBLISHING COMPANY
1911

FOREWORD

BY THE AUTHOR'S DAUGHTER

The following brief historical study is a fragment of a work which was intended to cover the operations against Charleston from their beginning to their consummation. The author, General Samuel Jones, late of the Army of the Confederate States, died before its completion and before he had reached the consideration of his own services in the defense of Charleston. The work is published from an unfinished manuscript left among the author's papers, and after the lapse of a number of years. It is offered now in the belief that it will be found of value and interest to the student of military history.

General Samuel Jones was born December 17, 1819, at Woodfield, the plantation home of his parents, in Powhatan County, Virginia. His father, Samuel Jones, was a nephew and ward of Governor William Giles, of Virginia, under whose care he was brought up, and a graduate of Princeton College. General Jones' mother was Ann Moseley, daughter of Mr. Edward Moseley, of Powhatan County. General Jones was appointed a cadet at West Point Military Academy from Virginia July 1, 1837, and was graduated and promoted to brevet second lieutenant July 1, 1841, and to be second lieutenant in the Second Artillery September 28, 1841. His first duty was on the Maine frontier, at Houlton, pending the Disputed Territory controversy. He was on duty at West Point, 1846-51, as assistant professor of mathematics and assistant instructor in artillery and infantry tactics. He was appointed assistant to the Judge Advocate of the Army at Washington and continued in the discharge of the duties of his position until he resigned his commission in the Army of the United States April 27, 1861. On May 1, 1861, he was made Major of Artillery in the military force of Virginia and later promoted to be Colonel. On July 22, 1861, he was made Chief of Artillery and Ordnance of the Army of Northern Virginia. He served on the staff of General Beauregard at the first battle of Manassas, and was promoted to be Brigadier General July 22, 1861, and appointed to the command of the brigade of General Bartow, which had lost its gallant commander on the field of Manassas. (The brigade consisted of the Seventh, Eighth, Ninth and Eleventh Georgia, and the Fourth Kentucky Regiments of Infantry and Alberto's Artillery.) On January 22, 1862, General Jones was appointed to the command of the department of which Pensacola was the headquarters. He was promoted to be Major General May 10, 1862, and on September 23, 1862, was assigned to the command of the Department of East Tennessee. From April to October, 1864, he was in command of the Department of South Carolina, Georgia, and Florida, and from January to May, 1865, of the Department of Florida and South Georgia. Here he made one of the last stands of the Confederacy, and held his position until the surrender at Appomattox.

General Jones was an accomplished soldier and gentleman, proficient in the sciences which entered into his military education, ardently attached to his profession of arms, and true to its highest ideals of conduct. In private life he possessed in a high degree the qualities which win and keep affection and esteem.

EMILY READ JONES.

WASHINGTON, D. C.,
September 2, 1911.

CONTENTS

THE SIEGE OF CHARLESTON

CHAPTER I

Ordinance of Secession—South Carolina Secedes—Fort Moultrie dismantled—Major Anderson transfers command to Fort Sumter—South Carolina takes possession of Fort Moultrie and Castle Pinckney—*Star of the West* fired on—Dissensions in President's Cabinet—Virginian Peace Conferences—Inauguration of Lincoln as President—Shall Sumter be evacuated?

When, on the 20th of December, 1860, the representatives of the people of South Carolina, in convention assembled, passed by a unanimous vote an Ordinance of Secession dissolving the connection of that State with the Government of the United States, Charleston which for a long time had been one of the most important seaports on the Atlantic coast of America, became a point of increased interest and solicitude both in this country and abroad.

Of the constitutional questions involved in the act of secession it is no part of the writer's purpose to treat. He proposes to give with the circumstances leading to them only a connected narrative of the principal military and naval operations against Charleston and on the South Atlantic coast which followed the secession of South Carolina and ten other Southern States.

Immediately on the withdrawal of South Carolina from the Union,—indeed for many weeks before the passage of the Ordinance of Secession,—the condition of the military defenses of Charleston harbor became most naturally a question of grave importance. At that time Fort Moultrie, on Sullivan's Island, was the only one of the forts constructed for the defense of the harbor that was occupied by United States troops. It was garrisoned by Companies E and H of First Regiment United States Artillery, Major Robert Anderson, of that regiment, commanding, the aggregate force present being less than eighty men.

When Congress met in December it was generally understood that the convention of the people of South Carolina which had been called to meet at Columbia on the 17th would surely and speedily pass an Ordinance of Secession. In anticipation of that event the representatives in Congress from that State called upon the President, Mr. Buchanan, and assured him that their State would in no way molest the forts until time and opportunity could be had for the consideration and amicable adjustment of all questions growing out of the altered relations between the State and general government, provided the latter would not in the meantime send reinforcements to, or change the military status in, the harbor of Charleston. The President declined to give any formal pledge in regard to the course he would pursue, but it is claimed, on what authority

need not be stated here, that he approved of the
suggestions, and that an informal understanding was
arrived at to the effect that the military status in
Charleston harbor should remain unchanged pending negotiations for the amicable adjustment of all
questions relating to public property, including the
forts within the limits of the State.   And to the end
that there might be no needless delay in the settlement of those important questions, one of the first
acts of the convention after passing the Ordinance
of Secession was to depute Mr. Robert W. Barnwell, Mr. James H. Adams, and Hon. James L.
Orr, eminent citizens of the State, to proceed to the
city of Washington "to treat with the Government
of the United States for the delivery of the forts,
magazines, lighthouses, and other real estate, with
their appurtenances, within the limits of South Carolina, and also for an apportionment of the public
debt, and for a division of all other property held
by the Government of the United States, as agents
of the Confederated States, of which South Carolina was recently a member; and generally to nego-
tiate as to all other measures and arrangements
proper to be made and adopted in the existing rela-
tion of the parties, and for the continuance of peace
and amity between this Commonwealth and the Government at Washington."

On the 11th of December, a few days after the
interview between the President and the representatives of South Carolina, instructions were sent
from the War Department to Major Anderson, in
accordance with the understanding claimed to have

been agreed on. They were in substance that he should carefully avoid every act which would needlessly tend to provoke aggression, and to that end he was instructed, not without evident and imminent necessity to occupy any position which could be construed into the assumption of a hostile attitude. At the same time he was ordered to hold possession of the forts in the harbor, and if attacked "to defend himself to the last extremity," or, as subsequently modified, "as long as any reasonable hope remained of saving the fort." His force was obviously too small to occupy more than one of the three forts in the harbor, but an attack on, or attempt to take possession of, any one he should regard as an act of hostility, and in that event he was authorized to occupy that one of the forts which in his judgment could be most easily defended. He was further authorized to take this precautionary measure whenever he might have tangible evidence of a design on the part of the authorities of South Carolina to proceed to any hostile act.

Those instructions are such as are not infrequently given by a military superior to an inferior, when the former has not, or does not choose to express, a clear and distinct purpose as to what is to be done by the latter. In such cases the instructions are so worded as in any event to shield the one who gives, and throw the responsibility of action on the one who has to execute them.

It was as well known at the War Department as to Major Anderson, that Fort Sumter could at that time be more easily and securely held than could

Fort Moultrie. If Major Anderson had remained at Moultrie, the weaker post, and had he been attacked, and his post captured, he would have been liable to censure under his instructions. Under the same instructions, if he abandoned the weaker and occupied the stronger fort, he thereby became open to censure for taking a "position which could be construed into the assumption of a hostile attitude."

Major Anderson was in the embarrassing position which besets a soldier "when the bugle gives an uncertain sound." He ardently desired to avoid, if possible, a hostile collision, and he believed—or apprehended—that a collision would occur if he remained at Fort Moultrie. He was a well trained and tried soldier, and an accomplished gentleman, with a high and scrupulous sense of honor. He acted as might have been expected of such an officer so circumstanced.

On the morning of the 27th of December Charleston and Washington and the whole country were startled by the announcement that during the preceding night Major Anderson had dismantled Fort Moultrie, spiked the guns, burned the carriages, cut down the flagstaff, and transferred his little command to Fort Sumter. An explanation of his course was immediately demanded by the Secretary of War, and as promptly given. Anderson replied that he had reason to believe the authorities of South Carolina designed to proceed to a hostile act. He abandoned Fort Moultrie because he was certain that if attacked, his garrison would be sacrificed and the command of the harbor lost. He had spiked his guns and burned their carriages to prevent their being used against himself; that if attacked, his garrison would never have surrendered without a fight; and he had felt it to be his solemn duty to remove his command from a fort which he could not probably hold longer than forty-eight or sixty hours, to one in which his power of resistance was greatly increased. And he might have added, if it would have been respectful, that he could hold Sumter long enough to give the Administration time to decide on the course it would pursue in the critical emergency and assume the responsibility which properly belonged to it instead of devolving it on one of its subordinate officers.

This act of Major Anderson produced serious complications both in the political and military States. The government of South Carolina, regarding it as a violation of the pledge, expressed or implied, to maintain the *status quo,* immediately took possession of Fort Moultrie and Castle Pinckney and other public property. And the political excitement throughout the country was greatly heightened.

As yet South Carolina was the only State which had seceded, and it was by no means certain that she would not continue to be alone in that movement. The course of Major Anderson and the attitude assumed by the Government in Washington went far toward precipitating secession in other States. Its effect in Georgia was quickly manifested. There was a fort—Pulaski—at the entrance to the Savannah River which was not garrisoned, but in the care of an ordnance sergeant. What more probable, judging by what had just occurred in Charleston harbor, than that the Government of the United States would speedily throw a garrison into Fort Pulaski and thus close the entrance from the sea to Savannah in the event of the secession of Georgia? Excitement ran high in the State, especially in Savannah. Governor Brown of that State had in the previous November called a convention of the people of the State to meet on the 16th of January, but long before the convention could meet the fort which commanded the approach to the chief city of the State would be occupied by United States troops unless steps were taken to prevent it. Assurances came from trusted representatives in Washington that the United States Government would resort to coercive measures, and produced the profoundest sensation. Notwithstanding that the State was still in the Union and its ultimate secession extremely doubtful, leading citizens of Savannah had resolved to seize Fort Pulaski without waiting for the assembling of the convention and its doubtful action, or for the sanction of the Executive of the State. Somewhat more moderate counsel, however, prevailed, and it was agreed to await the action of the Governor, who, on an urgent request from the Mayor of Savannah, hastened to that city, where he arrived on the evening of January 2. Late in the night, and after mature deliberation, he ordered Colonel Alexander R. Lawton, commanding the First Georgia Volunteers, to take possession of Fort Pulaski, "and to hold it against all persons, to be abandoned only under orders from me or under compulsion by an overpowering hostile force."[1]

The next day Colonel Lawton, with detachments of the Chatham Artillery (Captain Claibourne), the Savannah Volunteer Guard (Captain Scrivin), and the Oglethorp Light Infantry (Captain Bartow),[2] numbering about one hundred and twenty-five men, took formal possession of the fort without opposition, in the name of the State of Georgia.

Fuel was added to the fire by the sailing from New York on January 5, under instructions from the Headquarters of the Army, of the steamer *Star of the West*, with two hundred men, Lieutenant Charles R. Wood, Ninth United States Infantry, commanding, to reinforce and provision Fort Sumter. The *Star of the West* arrived off the bar of Charleston harbor late in the night of the 8th, and early in the morning crossed the bar and proceeded up the main channel toward Sumter, the Union ensign flying from the flagstaff. She was warned off by shots fired across her bow from a battery at Cumming's Point, but, disregarding the warning, she ran up a large United States flag at her fore and proceeded on her course, when the fire was directed at her, three shots striking her. The vessel then came about and steamed away, to New York.

---

[1] The Governor's order was in writing, and is of interest as a part of the history of the terms. See Appendix.

[2] Killed at first battle of Manassas.

The Cabinet was hopelessly divided in opinion. The Secretary of State had resigned because the President would not send reinforcements to Charleston. The Secretary of War, regarding Major Anderson's movement as a breach of faith with the representatives of South Carolina, resigned because the President would not withdraw the troops from Fort Sumter and from the harbor of Charleston. Startling events followed one another rapidly. In quick succession the States of Mississippi, Florida, Alabama, Georgia, and Louisiana seceded from the Union. A congress of representatives of those States assembled at Montgomery, Ala., on February 4 and inaugurated a new government, giving to it the name of "The Confederate States of America," which was soon joined by other Southern States.

It is difficult at this day to conceive the excitement and anxiety that pervaded Washington city during that eventful winter and spring. The lobbies of the hotels and of the Capitol and the galleries of the two houses of Congress were thronged with eager crowds discussing, or listening to the discussions of, the all-absorbing question of the day. As State after State seceded, and it was known that its representatives in Congress would rise in their places to announce the fact and withdraw, anxious crowds poured into the Capitol, and long before the hour of meeting of the houses the galleries were packed to the extent that it was difficult to escape from them before the adjournment, which was often far into the night.

To no class in the country were the passing events

of more absorbing and vital interest than to the officers of the Army and Navy who were natives and citizens of the Southern States. They could but watch with feverish anxiety the march of events which they were powerless to influence, though so nearly concerned in, and which were hastening rapidly and inevitably to a result which most of them unquestionably deeply deplored. Many of them, as their States seceded, resigned their commissions and returned to their homes in the South. Their resignations were accepted, and they left the old service and joined the new, unmolested by the Federal authorities, no one at that day openly impugning their honor and integrity for pursuing the path to which, in their judgment, duty and honor prompted.

Probably the preponderance of opinion at the time was that a disruption of the Union was inevitable and would be effected without war—when a Southern and Northern republic would exist side by side for a time, but a brief time; that when party rancor which then raged so fiercely subsided and it should become obvious that the mutual interests of the different sections were more potent than the questions which unhappily antagonized and divided them the two would come together again in a new and more satisfactory union under one government and one flag.

In the meantime good and patriotic men in all sections of the country, statesmen in the better sense of the term, as distinct from mere party politicians, were throwing oil on the troubled waters and striving with all their might to bring about an amicable adjustment of all questions in dispute, to avert, if possible, the calamities of war, which the course of fanatics and party politicians in both sections, who prized party ascendancy above the public weal, had for years tended to bring upon the country.

To this end a Peace Conference assembled in Washington on February 4. It originated in the General Assembly of Virginia, which, deprecating secession, invited the other States to send commissioners to meet five of her own most eminent citizens, "to consider, and, if practicable, agree upon some suitable adjustment of the questions which were then rending the Union asunder." Twenty-one States— seven slave-holding and fourteen non-slave-holding —were represented. It was presided over by the venerable Ex-President John Tyler, and contained many eminent and patriotic citizens of the States represented. A plan of adjustment was agreed upon, which it was earnestly hoped would prove satisfactory to all concerned. It was reported in both houses of Congress, but the withdrawal from that body of the representatives of six States had left one party largely in the ascendancy, and the plan proposed by the Peace Conference was rejected, not without manifestations of contempt.

President Buchanan succeeded in tiding over the few remaining days of his administration without bringing on a war between the States.

One of his last acts was to intimate indirectly through a distinguished Senator—Mr. Hunter of Virginia, to Mr. Davis, President of the Southern Confederacy—that he would be pleased to receive in Washington a commissioner or commissioners from the Confederate Government, and would lay before the Senate any communication that might be made through them. On this invitation Mr. Crawford of Georgia, Mr. Forsyth of Alabama, and Mr. Roman of Louisiana were appointed special commissioners to represent the Confederate States in Washington.

On the 4th of March, just one month after the Government of the Confederate States had been established and put in operation, Mr. Lincoln was inaugurated as President of the United States. All eyes were eagerly directed to the new President with the most anxious solicitude, as to the course he would pursue under the complicated and embarrassing circumstances that surrounded him.

The representatives of the Confederacy were not formally and officially received by the President, but in a few days after the inauguration they were, through the agency of two Justices of the Supreme Court,—Justices Nelson of New York and Campbell of Alabama,—in communication with Mr. Seward and other members of President Lincoln's Cabinet.

The all-important question, What should be the relations between the United States and the Confederated States? seemed to depend on the course which the former would pursue in regard to Fort Sumter. If the troops were withdrawn and amicable relations maintained, it was believed that the eight remaining slave-holding States would remain in the Union, and time and the efforts of lovers of the Union throughout the whole country might develop some satisfactory solution of the political conflict. If, however, an attempt were made to throw reinforcements and provisions into Sumter, thus manifesting a purpose to coerce the States which had seceded, a hostile collision would ensue, and some—perhaps all—of the remaining slave-holding States would secede and join the Southern Confederacy. Unquestionably a vast majority of intelligent men in the Southern States believed, without the shadow of a doubt, that any and every State of the Union possessed an inherent and reserved right to secede for cause, and that it rested with a convention of the people of the State, duly convened, to decide absolutely when a cause had arisen. Probably a majority of the same people believed that no sufficient cause had at that time arisen. An attempt, however, to coerce into the Union a State which had seceded, thus converting a union of consent into one of force, would be generally regarded as so radical and dangerous an infringement of the rights of the States as not only to justify, but to demand, secession as the only adequate mode and measure of redress.

Eminent gentlemen high in official position, zealous in devotion to the Union, whose opinions and counsel were entitled to weight, strongly advised the evacuation of Fort Sumter. Among them were Lieutenant General Scott, General-in-Chief of the Army, and General Totten, Chief of Engineers.

The President, in great doubt and perplexity as to the best course to pursue in regard to Fort Sumter, addressed the following brief note to the Secretary of War:

EXECUTIVE MANSION, March 15, 1861.
To THE HONORABLE SECRETARY OF WAR.

Dear Sir: Assuming it to be possible to now provision Fort Sumter, under all the circumstances is it wise to attempt it? Please give me your opinion in writing on this question.

Your obedient servant,

A. LINCOLN.

The Secretary replied that he had been most reluctantly forced to the conclusion that it would be unwise to make such an attempt. His opinion was based on those of the army officers who had expressed themselves on the subject, including the General-in-Chief of the Army, the Chief of Engineers, and all of the officers then within Fort Sumter, whose written opinions the Secretary embodied in his answer. The plan proposed by Mr. G. V. Fox, late of the navy, would, he said, be entitled to his favorable consideration if he "did not believe that the attempt to carry it into effect would initiate a bloody and protracted conflict. No practical benefit will result to the country or the Government by accepting the proposal alluded to, and I am therefore of the opinion that the cause of humanity and the highest obligation to the public interest would be best promoted by adopting the counsels of those brainy and experienced men whose suggestions I have laid before you."

General Scott, who six weeks previously had strenuously opposed the evacuation of Fort Sumter and had urged that it be reinforced, had under the altered aspect of affairs changed his opinion. To attempt it now would, in his opinion, require, in

addition to the means already at command, a fleet
of war vessels,—which could not be assembled in
less than four months,—five thousand additional
regular troops, and twenty thousand volunteers. To
organize such a force, even if undertaken immediately and without the sanction of Congress,—
which was not then in session,—could not in his
opinion be done in less than six or eight months.
"As a practical military question," he said, "the time
for succoring Fort Sumter, with any means at hand,
had passed away nearly a month ago. Since then
a surrender under assault or from starvation has
been merely a question of time."   The abandonment of the fort in a few weeks he regarded as a
sure necessity, and since it must be done "the sooner,
the more graceful on the part of the government."
He went further, and advised the abandonment of
Fort Pickens, at the entrance to the harbor of Pensacola; and, in addition to the military reasons assigned for this course, added the further reason that
"our Southern friends are clear that the evacuation
of both the forts would instantly soothe and give
confidence to the eight remaining slave-holding States
and render their cordial adherence to this Union
perpetual."

The same views were most forcibly presented by
General Totten, Chief of Engineers, in a memo-
randum read by him before the President and Cabinet on March 15 in the presence of General Scott,
Commander Stringham, and Mr. Fox. And again
on April 3 General Totten, impelled by a profound
sense of duty and "under the strongest convictions

on some military questions upon which great political events seem about to turn," urged the same views in regard to both Forts Sumter and Pickens in a letter to the Secretary of War, in which he said: "In addition to what I have heretofore said as to the impracticability of efficiently re-enforcing and supplying this fort [Sumter], I will now say only that if the fort was fitted with men and munitions it could hold out but a short time. It would be obliged to surrender with loss of life, for it would be bravely and obstinately defended, and the greater the crowd within, the greater the proportionate loss. This issue can be averted only by sending a large army and navy to capture all the surrounding forts and batteries, and to assemble and apply these there is now no time. If we do not evacuate Fort Sumter it will be wrested from us by force." He added in conclusion: "Having no personal ambition or party feeling to lead or mislead me to conclusions, I have maturely studied the subject as a soldier bound to give all his faculties to his country, which may God preserve in peace."

The Hon. Stephen A. Douglas, the popular leader of a large party whose ardent love for the Union no one could question, had introduced in the Senate a resolution advising the withdrawal of the troops from all forts within the Southern Confederacy, except those at Key West and the Dry Tortugas; and urged its passage in an earnest speech. Deeply as he deplored the establishment of the Southern Confederacy, its existence *de facto* he declared could not be denied, and it was entitled to the forts within its limits.   He was the leader of a party, and spoke by authority.   "I proclaim boldly," he said, "the policy of those with whom I act.   We are for peace."

The Secretary of State, Mr. Seward, himself impressed upon the President and commissioners of the Southern Confederacy, through the agency of Justices Campbell and Nelson of the Supreme Court, that no attempt would be made by the United States Government to reinforce or revictual Fort Sumter, and that the then existing military status in Charleston harbor should not be changed in any way prejudicial to the Southern Confederacy.   He authorized Justice Campbell to write, as he did, to Mr. Davis, that before the receipt of his letter he (Mr. Davis) would have learned by telegraph that the order for the evacaution of Fort Sumter had been given.   On April 7, no such order having yet been given, and certain military and naval preparations which it was well known the United States Government was making having caused much feverish apprehension, Justice Campbell addressed a letter to Mr. Seward, asking if the assurances the latter had given him were well or ill-founded, to which Mr. Seward replied: "Faith as to Sumter fully kept—wait and see." When that last assurance was given Lieutenant Talbot, of the army, and Mr. Chew, confidential messengers for the War and State departments, were speeding away to Charleston, bearing to the Governor of South Carolina and to Major Anderson assurances that Sumter would be speedily revictualed.

The Peace Conference, and all who were laboring for peace, had failed to accomplish the purpose so ardently desired. Other and more potent influences were at work, which influences frustrated and brought to naught all efforts to attain an amicable adjustment of the political complications.

CHAPTER II

Pending the informal negotiations for peace, plans
were devised and preparations made to reinforce
and revictual Fort Sumter. Captain G. V. Fox, late
of the United States Navy, and Colonel Lawson,
both confidential agents of the Government, had at
different times passed from Washington through
Charleston to Sumter, and returned, ostensibly for
the purpose of arranging with Major Anderson the
details for the evacuation; but really, as subsequently
appeared, to ascertain by personal observation the
practicability and expediency of reinforcing and re-
victualing the fort. Captain Fox intimated to Major
Anderson the purpose of his visit, but made no
definite arrangement with him, nor even disclosed to
him his plans. Finally on the 8th of April Lieutenant Talbot and Mr. Chew, the confidential agents
of the War and State departments at Washington,
arrived in Charleston with assurances for Major
Anderson, which they were not permitted to deliver,
that if he could hold out until the 12th his garrison

would be reinforced and supplied; and before leaving Charleston, on the same date, they informed Governor Pickens and the Confederate general commanding that the Government would provision Fort Sumter,—peaceably, if possible; forcibly, if necessary.

The decision of the Government to reinforce and revictual Sumter was communicated to Major Anderson in a letter sent through the mail, and dated April 4. Replying through the Adjutant Major, Anderson expressed great surprise at the receipt of the information, coming as it did so quickly after and positively contradicting the assurances which Mr. Crawford had telegraphed he was authorized to make. It was too late then, he said, to offer any advice in regard to Captain Fox's plan—then in process of execution—for the relief of the fort. He doubted the practicability of the plan, but whether the attempt should succeed or fail, the result he was sure would be most deplorable. He ought, he modestly said, to have been informed that the expedition was to sail. On the contrary, he had gathered from his conversation with the Government's confidential messenger, Colonel Lawson, that the plan hinted at by Captain Fox would not be attempted, and he concludes: "We shall strive to do our duty, though I frankly say that my heart is not in this war which I see is to be thus commenced."

On the 5th and 6th of April the Confederate commissioners then in Washington telegraphed Mr. Toombs, Secretary of State of the Confederate States, that active preparations were in progress to dispatch troops and supplies to sea, conveyed by war vessels. It was rumored that the expedition was to sail for San Domingo, but Charleston was believed to be its real destination. The New York *Tribune* of April 11 announced that the main object of the expedition was the relief of Sumter, and that a force would be landed which would overcome all opposition. That announcement was promptly telegraphed to the government at Montgomery and the authorities in Charleston.

On the 10th the Confederate Secretary of War instructed the general commanding in South Carolina that if he felt confident that Mr. Chew had been properly authorized to announce the purpose of the United States Government to provision Fort Sumter, he would at once demand the surrender of the fort; and, if refused, proceed to reduce it. In the meantime the naval expedition which had been fitted out in New York had gone to sea and was steaming for Charleston harbor.

Major Anderson had carried with him from Moultrie to Sumter only about three months' supply of food, and the garrison would of necessity capitulate when it had consumed that supply, provided it were not revictualed. That could only be done by vessels passing in through one of the channels. Batteries had been erected along the channel shore of Morris Island to guard the main channel, and on Sullivan's Island to guard Maffit's Channel. Preparations had also been made, with all the care and dispatch that could be employed, for the reduction of Sumter if, unhappily, it should become necessary to resort to force. These preparations were of such a nature as to leave little doubt of the speedy accomplishment of that purpose when the emergency should arise.

Brigadier General Beauregard, assigned to command of the military forces in and around Charleston, entered on that duty early in the first week of March. He made some modifications of and additions to the works already constructed and in course of construction. There were batteries at Fort Johnson, an old dilapidated work on James Island,—at and near Cumming's Point, the northern extremity of Morris Island. Sullivan's Island was further strengthened by mortar batteries to the east of Fort Moultrie, and its western end by a masked battery to enfilade the channel front of Sumter. There was also a floating battery of long-range guns off the western end of Sullivan's Island, designed by and constructed under the direction of Captain John Randolph Hamilton, late an officer of the United States Navy. The guns of Fort Moultrie had been repaired and remounted and were in readiness for action. There were mortar batteries near Mount Pleasant on the mainland to the northward in Christ Church parish, and at Castle Pinckney, between Sumter and the city. At Cumming's Point, thirteen hundred yards from Sumter, was a battery of long-range guns, among them the first Blakely rifle gun ever used in this country—a present to South Carolina from Mr. Charles K. Prioleau, of Charleston, which had just arrived from England. Near this was an ironclad land battery, devised and constructed by Mr. (afterward General) C. H. Stevens, of Charleston, a line of ten detached batteries of two guns each stretched along the channel front of Morris Island. To light up the channel at night lest vessels might attempt to enter unperceived, two strong Drummond lights were established at suitable points—one on Morris, the other on Sullivan's Island. The lights were purchased in New York and arrived in Charleston in the latter part of March or early in April. Fort Sumter was thus encircled by a line of batteries varying in distance from 1300 to 2450 yards, and mounting thirty guns and seventeen mortars, in readiness for action. The batteries were manned mainly by the First South Carolina Regular Artillery and detachments of the First Regular Infantry and volunteer artillery companies. Colonel Maxey Gregg's regiment—First South Carolina Volunteers—was on Morris Island and had charge of the channel batteries. Colonel Petagrew's Rifle Regiment and the Charleston Light Dragoons guarded the eastern part of Sullivan's Island. General James Simons commanded on Morris Island, the batteries there being under the immediate command of Lieutenant Colonel DeSaussure. General R. G. M. Dunovant commanded on Sullivan's Island, the batteries then being under the immediate command of Lieutenant Colonel R. S. Ripley, formerly of the United States Artillery, Captain Ransom Calhoun commanding Fort Moultrie. Captain Hollanquist commanded the masked or enfilading battery near the west end of Sullivan's Island. Captain Hamilton commanded the floating battery of his own construction, and a Dahlgren gun near by. Captain Martin commanded the mortar battery near Mount Pleasant, and Captain George S. Thomas that at Fort Johnson.

Probably no more novel military force ever before assembled under arms for actual service than that assembled for the defense of Charleston at that time. The Ordinance of Secession which had been passed by a unanimous vote of the representatives of the people in convention assembled was sustained with great unanimity by the mass of the people in person, and by a lavish expenditure of private means. Gentlemen of wealth contributed liberally to arm and equip the volunteers who were called into the service. Some of them placed companies and battalions in the field. A gentleman long past the period of life when military service may be exacted of the citizen, was seen walking post as a sentinel on Morris Island. He had at his own cost armed and equipped a company and then given the command of it to a younger brother, serving himself as a private in the ranks. Gentlemen, the owners of large landed estates, served with their sons and nephews as privates in the ranks, toiled with the pick and shovel side by side with their own negro slaves in the construction of earthwork and in the various other laborious work incident to life in camp in active service.

Fort Sumter, when occupied by Major Anderson, was in an unfinished condition, and for many days afterwards—in the opinion of Captain (now General) Doubleday, an officer of the garrison—might have been easily captured by escalade. It was not, however, the policy of South Carolina,—or later of the Southern Confederacy,—to proceed to any hostile act while negotiations were in progress for the peaceable possession of the fort. The little garrison labored diligently in mounting guns and putting it in condition to secure it from assault. In a short time forty-eight guns of calibers from twenty-four pounds to ten-inch columbiads were mounted and ready for action. In addition, one ten- and four eight-inch columbiads were arranged on the parade, to be used as mortars to throw shells into Charleston and on Cumming's Point. The garrison consisted of six commissioned officers and seventy-three enlisted men. There were also three officers and forty mechanics and employees of the Corps of Engineers. The commissioned officers were Robert Anderson, Captain Abner Doubleday, Captain Truman Seymour, First Lieutenant Jefferson C. Davis, Second Lieutenant Norman I. Hall, all of the First Regiment of Artillery; Captain J. G. Foster and Lieutenants G. W. Snyder and R. K. Meade, United States Engineers; and Assistant Surgeon S. W. Crawford, United States Army.

On the afternoon of April 11 General Beauregard sent to Major Anderson by three of his aides-de-camp —Captain Stephen D. Lee, Ex-Senator James Chesnut, and Lieutenant A. R. Chisholm—a formal demand for the immediate surrender of Fort Sumter, with the offer to allow him to take from the fort all company arms and property and all private property —he with his officers and men to be transported to any port in the United States that he might designate, and to salute his flag on lowering it. Major Anderson replied in writing, declining in appropriate terms to comply with the demand, but said verbally to the officers who bore the summons: "I will await the first shot, and if you do not batter us to pieces we will be starved out in a few days." His reply was telegraphed to the Confederate Secretary of War, who, seizing upon the last informal verbal expression as opening a possible way of escape from a resort to force, instructed General Beauregard to inform Major Anderson that if he would designate a reasonable time when he would evacuate the fort, and agree in the meantime not to use his guns against Charleston or its defenses, fire would not be opened on Sumter. To this offer Major Anderson replied carefully and guardedly as to the terms, that if provided with suitable means of transportation he would evacuate the fort at noon on the 15th "should I not receive prior to that time contrary instructions from my Government, or additional supplies." He would not in the meantime use his guns against the Confederates unless compelled to do so by some hostile act against "this fort or the flag of my Government by the Confederate forces or any part of them; or by the commission of some act manifesting a hostile purpose against the fort or the flag." The reply was equivalent to a refusal of the offer, because General Beauregard and Major Anderson had ample reason for believing that an expedition for the relief of Sumter had sailed from New York and was then within a few miles of Charleston harbor, and would not be allowed to enter if it could be prevented. Colonel Chesnut, the bearer of the message, therefore formally notified Major Anderson, by authority of his chiefs, that fire would be opened on Sumter in one hour. It was then twenty minutes past three o'clock A. M.

At half-past four o'clock on Friday, April 12, Captain George S. James, at Fort Johnson, on an order from Captain Stephen D. Lee, of General Beauregard's staff, aimed and fired the first shell, which fell, bursting, on the parade ground of Fort Sumter.

It was the initial shot of the war, the first harsh note of a réveille which called the gunners to their posts, and before five o'clock the whole circle of batteries was in active play on the majestic fort in the center. For nearly two hours Sumter remained silent; then about seven o'clock opened; the bombardment became general and continued throughout the day. The effect of the fire on Sumter was plainly visible. The vertical fire from the mortar batteries was surprisingly accurate, and so effective that the barbet guns, which were of the heaviest caliber, were soon abandoned, several having been dismounted by the long-range guns, and the fire from the fort was confined to the casemate guns. Fire was maintained with spirit and effect, and directed mainly against Cumming's Point, Fort Moultrie, and the batteries near and to the west of it. At night the fire from Sumter ceased, only to husband the scant supply of ammunition. At the commencement of the action there were but seven hundred cartridges in the fort.

All blankets, company clothing not in use, and hospital bedding were cut up to be converted into cartridge bags, and men, when not at the guns, diligently stitched through the long day and night—with the only six needles in the fort—in the preparation of cartridges. The Confederate fire slackened, but continued slowly, and, mingling with the uproar of a storm of wind and rain which prevailed, dropped shells on the fort at intervals of about fifteen minutes through the night.

There was no bread or flour in the fort, and in the gray dawn the garrision breakfasted on salt pork and a scant remnant of rice sifted as well as practicable from fragments of broken window glass which an accident had mingled with it.

Early in the afternoon of the 12th three war vessels had been seen off the bar, where they were joined by others early in the morning of the 13th. The presence of the fleet bearing, as was well known, reinforcements and supplies incited both the assailants and defenders of the fort to increased activity. The Confederate fire was resumed at early dawn with greater rapidity and accuracy than during the previous day. During the morning Lieutenant Alfred Rhett had been firing hot shot from thirty-two pounders in Moultrie, and with effect, as was soon manifested.[3]   About eight o'clock a small column of smoke was seen rising above the fort, and soon

[3]The officers' quarters had been set on fire the day before, but the upper cisterns having been pierced by shot, the water flooded the quarters and extinguished the fire.

increased to large volume over the officer's quarters, the roof of which had been penetrated by hot shot. It was impossible to extinguish the flames, which spread rapidly. The burning quarters were near the main magazine, which it was plain would be so encircled with fire as to make it necessary to close the doors—if even that would prevent an explosion. All officers and men not at the guns worked rapidly and with a zeal quickened by the imminence of the peril, to remove the powder, but the flames spread so rapidly that only fifty barrels were taken out and distributed through the casemates before the intense heat made it necessary to close the doors of the magazine and pack earth against them. The Confederate fire was quickened, and soon the whole range of officers' quarters was in flames. The wind carried the fire to the roof of the barracks and the hot shot dropping on the burning building increased the conflagration, which soon spread to both barracks. Dense clouds of smoke and cinders were driven by the wind into the casemates, the smoke blinding and stifling the men and the sparks setting fire to boxes and clothing huddled together. This made it perilous to keep the powder which had been rescued from the magazine at so much peril, and it was tumbled through the embrasure into the bay.

The fire reached the magazine of grenades arranged in the stairs, towers, and implement rooms, exploding the grenades, destroying the tower at the west gorge angle, and nearly destroying the other. The effect of the explosion, and the direct fire on the towers, was to damage and fill the stairways with débris so as to render it almost impossible to reach the terre-plein.

Amid the storm of fire from without and within the fire from the fort was most gallantly maintained. Filled with admiration of the pluck of the men who stood to their guns with such indomitable will when it seemed they were in imminent danger of being blown skyward by the explosion of thirty thousand pounds of powder in the magazines, many Confederates sprang to the parapets, and at every shot from the fort waved their hats and loudly cheered its brave defenders. About one o'clock the flagstaff, which had been repeatedly struck, fell. The flag was secured by Lieutenant Hall and hoisted on a temporary staff by Lieutenant Snyder and two laborers, Hart and Dosie of the Engineers. In the interval between the fall and hoisting of the flag General Beauregard dispatched three of his aides to the fort with an offer of assistance to extinguish the fire, which offer, however, was respectfully declined.

Seeing the flag down and believing the garrison to be in imminent peril, Ex-Senator Wigfall—one of General Beauregard's aides-de-camp who was with the troops on Morris Island—with the permission of General Simons pulled in a small boat, with one man, Private Gourdine Young of the Palmetto Guard, to Sumter. Being permitted to enter, he urged a suspension of hostilities, with a view to capitulation. He expressed to Major Anderson the high admiration his gallant defense had inspired in all who witnessed it, and assured him of the most honorable and liberal terms. Major Anderson acceded to the proposal, naming as his terms the same that had been offered him on the 11th, and the white flag was hoisted. In the meantime General Beauregard's aides, who had been dispatched with the offer of assistance, had arrived, and ascertaining from them that the visit of Senator Wigfall was not authorized by the general commanding, Major Anderson declared that he would immediately raise his flag again and renew the action, but consented to delay until General Beauregard could be communicated with. The brief negotiations resulted in the capitulation of the fort a little after dark, on the same terms which had been offered on the 11th.

With the exception of burning the quarters of the officers and men, a disaster which would not have occurred if they had been made originally fire-proof, the fort had sustained but little damage. The distance of the nearest breaching battery was thirteen hundred yards, too great for effective work with the guns then in use. The main gates had been destroyed, but they could readily have been built up with stone and rubbish. The quarters were for comfort, not for defensive purposes, and were an element of weakness from the beginning. When they had been burned without exploding the magazine, with sufficient labor the fort could have been made more defensible than it was when the action commenced. The obstacles in the way of a longer defense were the lack of cartridges and men. The men could have subsisted many days on the salt pork in store and would cheerfully have done so. But with a fleet bearing reinforcements and supplies in full view for

twenty-four hours without making an effort to reach
the fort, there was no encouragement to the garrison
to hold out in the hope of possible relief before the
alternative of starvation would compel a capitulation.

The war steamers *Powhatan, Pawnee,* and *Pocahontas,* the steamer transport *Baltic,* and three steam
tugs had been prepared to carry succor to Fort Sumter, and sailed from New York on the 9th and 10th.
The *Baltic,* which carried the reinforcements and
supplies, the *Pawnee,* and *Pocahontas* arrived off
Charleston, where they found the *Harriet Lane* early
on the morning of the 12th. The passage had been
stormy. One of the tugs was driven into Wilmington by stress of weather and neither of the others,
nor the *Powhatan,* arrived. The sea was running
high off Charleston, and Mr. Fox waited, but in
vain, for the *Powhatan* before attempting to enter.
That steamer was regarded as better constructed and
equipped for fighting than any other of the expedition, and carried, besides, the launches which were
to have been used to throw men and supplies into
Sumter. But it had been withdrawn from the expedition and its destination changed on the 7th without the knowledge of Mr. Fox, by the President,
at the instance of the Secretary of State. Captain
Rowan, of the *Pawnee,* seized an ice schooner, which
he placed at the disposal of Mr. Fox, who intended
to go in it with succor for the fort on the night of
the 13th, but before night set in the white flag was
hoisted over Sumter.

In the public mind some odium attached to the
commandery of the naval expedition for failing to

attempt to throw the reinforcements and supplies into Sumter. The concurrent opinion, however, of the officers within the fort and of others whose duties required of them careful study of the situation, was that any persistent attempt to accomplish the proposed object would not only have failed, but would have ended disastrously.

It had been agreed between General Beauregard and Major Anderson that the Union garrison should evacuate the fort the next day, as soon as the necessary preparations could be made. A steamer would carry the garrison to any port in the United States that Major Anderson might designate, or transfer it to one of the vessels then off the harbor. Major Anderson preferred the latter course.

While saluting the flag one man, Private Daniel Hough, was instantly killed, one Private Edward Galway mortally, and four severely wounded by the premature discharge of a gun and the explosion of a pile of cartridges. The Confederate commander ordered that the unfortunate man who had been killed should be buried with military honors, and the wounded properly cared for. At four o'clock P. M. on Sunday the 14th the Union garrison marched out, colors flying and the band playing "Yankee Doodle," and, embarking on the steamer *Isabel*, passed out over the bar, where it was transferred to the steamer *Baltic*, and sailed away for New York. As the *Isabel* passed through the channel the Confederate soldiers manifested their respect for Major Anderson and his gallant command by standing silent and uncovered in front of their batteries.

Lieutenant Colonel Roswell S. Ripley, commanding a battalion consisting of Captain Hollanquist's company of the First South Carolina Artillery, and the Palmetto Guard, Captain Cuthbert commanding, succeeded Major Anderson and the two companies of the First United States Artillery as the garrison of the fort. The Confederate and palmetto flags were hoisted side by side over Fort Sumter, and amid enthusiastic cheers saluted by the batteries around the harbor.

When the news of the bombardment and reduction of Sumter was flashed over the telegraphic wires the whole country was startled and electrified. The question of peace or war which had so long trembled in the balance was no longer doubtful. Hostilities had commenced. This was the beginning of a war in which before it closed the United States alone, in addition to a vast naval force, armed, equipped, and brought into the field nearly three millions of soldiers, of whom nearly, if not quite, four hundred thousand lost their lives in the service. How many were brought into the field by the Confederate States, and what the loss of life, will probably never be known. The knowledge has been lost with the cause they served.

CHAPTER III

The theater of the war which had virtually commenced in Charleston harbor on the 12th of April,
1861, was soon transferred to distant fields in other
States, and, with the exception of a blockading fleet
off her coast, South Carolina was for many months
exempt from the presence of a hostile force. Neither
party to the contest was prepared for war. Indeed,
for many weeks after the reduction of Fort Sumter
the country was not fully awake to the fact that war
on a gigantic scale had commenced. There was a
breach in the Union, and a hostile collision—happily
without the shedding of blood—had occurred in the
harbor of Charleston. Face to face with actual hostilities, those in the North charged with the conduct
of affairs might, it was hoped, pause to weigh well
and count the cost of a war to coerce into the Union
the States which had seceded and further to reflect
what would be the worth of a Union of States
"pinned together by bayonets," as Mr. Greely forcibly expressed and deprecated. The first battle of Ma-

47

nassas, or Bull Run, went far towards dispelling any expectation of an amicable settlement of the difficulties, but even after that event hope was cherished that the war would be very brief. Mr. Seward, Secretary of State of the United States, labored diligently to impress on the country, and on foreign governments through their diplomatic representatives, that the contest would be ended in sixty or ninety days. In the meantime preparations for war went forward rapidly. Early in August preparations were commenced for sending a combined land and naval expedition to some point on the South Atlantic coast. Admiral S. F. DuPont was selected to command the naval and Brigadier General T. W. Sherman the land forces, and the two in concert were charged with the organization of their respective commands.

The troops were furnished by Pennsylvania and New York and all of the New England States except Vermont. There were thirteen infantry regiments organized into three brigades, and of troops not brigaded, the First New York Engineers, Colonel Edward W. Sewell, Third Rhode Island Artillery (heavy), Colonel Nathaniel W. Brown, and Battery E, Third United States Artillery, Captain John Hamilton. The brigades were commanded respectively by Brigadier General Egbert L. Viele, Brigadier General I. I. Stevens and Brigadier General Horatio G. Wright. The organization was designated as "The Expeditionary Corps" and its aggregate strength the day before it sailed was twelve thousand six hundred and fifty-three (12,653).

The land and naval forces had assembled by October 22 in Hampton Roads, Va., where it was detained until the 29th by foul weather and the absence of some of the transports. Great precaution had been taken to keep its destination a profound secret, and it sailed under sealed orders. Nevertheless its destination was known to the Confederate Government and to the commanding general in South Carolina before it left the Capes of Virginia. Indeed, without direct information, it could scarcely have been doubted that it was destined for Port Royal, S. C., which was not only the best and most commodious port on the Atlantic coast south of the Capes of Virginia, but best situated as a base of operations both by land and water on the coasts of South Carolina, Georgia, and Florida.

The expedition, which consisted of fifty vessels, sailed on October 29, Flag Officer DuPont's flag flying over the steam frigate *Wabash*. It was the largest fleet that had ever sailed under the American flag. It had been preceded the day before by a fleet of twenty-five coal-laden schooners, convoyed by the sloop-of-war *Vandalia*, with orders in the event of parting company to rendezvous off the mouth of Savannah River.

When the fleet had cleared the Capes of Virginia, much care and time were expended in forming it into a double echelon line, and when that was accomplished it proceeded majestically on its course. On the morning of November 2 only one sail of all the vast naval armament was visible from the deck of the flagship *Wabash*. During the afternoon of the 1st rough weather set in, gradually increasing to a heavy gale from the southeast, and in the night it rose to a hurricane, scattering the fleet. During the 2d the weather moderated and the vessels began to heave in sight. Of the men-of-war the *Isaac Smith*, Lieutenant W. A. Nicholson commanding, one of the most efficient and best armed steamers of her class, had narrowly escaped foundering in the gale, throwing overboard her entire formidable battery. Thus relieved, she was enabled to go to the assistance of the steamer *Governor*, which was in a most critical condition, and in imminent peril of foundering. The *Governor* had on board a fine battalion of six hundred marines, Major I. G. Reynolds commanding. The most strenuous and heroic efforts of the commander and crew of the *Isaac Smith* to rescue the imperiled marines failed, but later the steam frigate *Sabine*, Captain Cadwallader Ringgold, commanding, came to the rescue. Every movable article on the *Governor* had been thrown overboard to lighten her, and the *Sabine* succeeded in rescuing from the wreck before it went down the crew and all of the marines except a corporal and six privates. Some of the transport steamers were lost and others were saved only by throwing overboard horses and cargoes. None of the troop transports were lost.

On the morning of the 4th the flagship and nearly all of the fleet were off the bars of Port Royal harbor, when, under Flag-officer DuPont's order, it was joined by the frigate *Saratoga*, Captain Sardoner, of the blockading fleet off Charleston. That evening and the next morning the war vessels and transports passed over the bar and anchored.

The coast line of Port Royal is such as to make it exceedingly difficult of defense by land batteries. The headlands on Hilton Head Island to the southward, and Bay Point to the northward, are nearly three miles apart. At so great a distance none but works of great strength, armed with guns of the heaviest caliber and longest range, could make any formidable opposition to the entrance of a powerful fleet. General Beauregard, relieved about the end of May from duty in South Carolina, before leaving had examined the coast and designated certain points at which defensive works should be constructed. The importance of Port Royal and the difficulties in the way of defending it were alike obvious.[1] He planned the works for the harbor and designated their armaments, which it was essential should be guns of the heaviest caliber for the water fronts. Under the direction of Major James H. Trapier, of the Engineers, and subsequently under the administration of Brigadier General Roswell S. Ripley, who was assigned to the command of the Military Department of South Carolina on the 21st of August, the works at the designated points were commenced, and the construction was pressed forward with all the means available. Major Francis D. Lee, of the South

[1]He advised that no attempt be made to construct works for its defense, but yielded to the urgent representations of the Governor of the State, with the condition that the works should be formidable in themselves and heavily armed.

Carolina Engineers, was charged with the construction of the work on Hilton Head, called Fort Walker, and Captain Gregory of one on Bay Point, called Fort Beauregard. They were not commenced until late in July, and were incomplete and not armed agreeably to the prescribed plan, because suitable guns could not be procured. Instead of seven ten-inch guns, as had been designated for the water front of Fort Walker, there was but one gun of that class. The other twenty-three guns mounted were of lighter caliber, two of them being twelve-pounders.

Brigadier General Thomas F. Drayton, a landed gentleman whose plantations were in the immediate vicinity, commanded the military district in which Port Royal was embraced. His brother, Captain Percival Drayton, commanded the Union steam sloop-of-war *Pocahontas.* The garrison of Fort Walker consisted of Companies A and B of the German Artillery, Captains D. Werner and H. Harmes; Company C, Ninth (afterwards the Eleventh) South Carolina Volunteers, Captain J. Bedon, manning the guns on the water front; all under command of Major A. M. Huger, First Artillery, South Carolina Militia. The flank and rear guns were manned by detachments from Captains Bedon's, Canaday's and White's companies, Ninth Volunteer Infantry. A reserve was commanded by Captain White. The entire force in the work numbered two hundred and twenty men, the whole commanded by Colonel John A. Wagner, First South Carolina Militia Artillery. The whole force on the island was 687 men. Across the channel and distant 2 5/8 miles from Fort

Walker, on Bay Point Island, was Fort Beauregard. It mounted nineteen guns of about the same class as those in Fort Walker, and was manned by two companies, the Beaufort Artillery, Captain Stephen Elliott, Jr., and Captain Harrison's Company of Infantry. Captain Elliott commanded the fort. Commodore Tattnall commanded three small river steamers which a single broadside from the flagship alone could probably have sunk.

On the 5th, while four of the Union war vessels were reconnoitering, a few shots were exchanged between them and the forts and Commodore Tattnall's steamboats, but with little damage to either side. On the 6th a heavy westerly wind prevailed, making it unadvisable to attack. The morning of the 7th was calm and bright, the water of the bay smooth, and with not a ripple to disturb the accuracy of fire.

Early in the morning signals from the flagship warned the commanders of the different war vessels more than four miles outside of a straight line connecting the positions of the two forts to form line and prepare for action. At the head of the main column was the flagship *Wabash*, Commander C. R. P. Rodgers, followed in the order named by the side-wheel steam frigate *Susquehanna*, Captain I. S. Sardoner; sloops-of-war *Mohican*, Commander S. W. Gordon; *Seminole*, Commander J. P. Gillis: *Pawnee*, Lieutenant Commander R. H. Wyman; and gunboats *Unadilla*, Lieutenant Commander Napoleon Collins; *Ottawa*, Lieutenant Commander Thomas H. Stephens; *Pembina*, Lieutenant Commander John P. Bankhead; and the sail sloop-of-war *Vandalia*, Commander Francis S. Haggerty, towed by the *Isaac Smith*, Lieutenant Commander J. W. A. Nicholson. The latter vessel, as has been stated, had thrown her guns overboard in the gale. In the flanking column and little more than a ship's length distant, were the *Bienville*, Commander Charles Steadman leading; the gunboats *Seneca*, Lieutenant Commander Daniel Ammen; *Penguin*, Lieutenant Commander P. A. Rudd, and the *Augusta*, Commander E. G. Parrott.

Flag-officer DuPont's plan of action, carried out with much precision, was to lead his main column—the different steamers something more than a ship's length apart—on an elliptical course, passing up the main channel at the distance of about eight hundred yards from Fort Walker, delivering their fire on that fort as long as the guns could be trained upon it; then turning seaward and approaching to within about six hundred yards, again deliver fire as long as the guns could be brought to bear. The operation was to be continued until the fort should be silenced. The flanking column delivered its fire on Fort Beauregard while passing up, then directed its attention to Commodore Tattnall's little river boats, which had steamed out of Beaufort River to take part in the action. The Flag-officer cautioned the commanders of his gunboats that he knew Tattnall well as an officer of courage and capacity, and it was highly probable that in the heat and smoke of battle he would endeavor to pass out and destroy the transports on which was General Sherman's Expeditionary Corps. If he attempted it, his steamboats must be destroyed. Tattnall's puny fleet was soon driven off, however, and took shelter in Skull Creek to the northwest. The gunboats then took favorable positions to the northward of Fort Walker, and while the main column moved slowly and majestically on its prescribed course, delivering a direct fire, the gunboats poured in a most destructive flank fire, all the more effective because the fort had not been provided with traverses. Later in the action the *Pocahontas,* Commander Percival Drayton, which had been delayed by injuries received in the gale, steamed into the harbor and taking suitable position opened on Fort Walker.

The majestic fleet continued to move on its course and deliver its fire with the regularity of machinery, and the skill and deliberate coolness of the officers and gunners, the weight and excellence of the armaments, and the glossy smoothness of the water, made the fire wonderfully accurate and destructive.

It was a most unequal conflict. The contrast between the batteries engaged was very marked. The fleet carried 150 guns, many of them of the heaviest and most approved pattern then in use; the ammunition and equipments were perfect of their kind, and the officers and men who directed and worked them were engaged in their legitimate occupation, to which they had been thoroughly trained. There were twenty guns of much lighter caliber mounted in Fort Walker,—against which the attack was mainly directed,—many of them hastily mounted on improvised carriages, not adapted to the guns, after the fleet appeared off the harbor, and the ammunition was defective. The manufacture of heavy ordnance and ammunition was almost an unknown industry in the South prior to the war. Probably there was not a man in Fort Walker who had been trained to the use of heavy guns. The commanding officer himself aimed and fired the first gun, and owing to defective fuse the shell burst near the muzzle. Some ammunition did not fit the guns,—the shells could not be driven home,—but they were nevertheless fired, with more risk to those who worked them than to those at whom they were aimed. The ten-inch gun, the heaviest and only one of the kind in the fort bounded from its carriage at the fourth or fifth discharge, and was useless during the remainder of the action. The twenty-four-pounder rifle was choked while ramming down a shell, and lay idle during the engagement. There was no gun on the flank to reply to the gunboats near the mouth of Fish Hall Creek, the thirty-two pounder on the right flank having been shattered by a shot early in the action. The inexperienced gunners at these very defective batteries were firing at steamers constantly in motion, and often beyond effective range of the guns.

General Drayton crossed over to Hilton Head early in the morning of the 5th, and assumed the general direction of affairs. Captain Stewart's Company of the Ninth South Carolina Regiment, which occupied a battery at Braddock's Point, the extreme southern point of the island, was ordered up to reinforce Captain Elliott at Battery Beauregard. But the order miscarried, the company did not move until the 7th, and its passage to Beauregard was intercepted by the Union gunboats. Late in the afternoon of the 6th 450 men of the Georgia Infantry, Captain Berry commanding, and Captain Read's Battery of two twelve-pounder howitzers and 50 men arrived. They had been sent by Brigadier General Lawton to reinforce the troops on Hilton Head. A little later Colonel DeSaussure's Regiment, the Fifteenth South Carolina Volunteers, 650 strong, arrived at Seabrook's Wharf on Skull Creek, and passed over to within supporting distance of Fort Walker. There were therefore on Hilton Head on the 7th about 1450 men, 220 of whom were in Fort Walker. They were there to defend the island against the Union fleet manned by full complements of men, and carrying 150 guns, a battalion of 600 marines, and General Sherman's Expeditionary Corps of 12,653—aggregate. The action commenced about nine o'clock in the morning and continued about four and a half hours. A few minutes' fire of the fleet convinced the most sanguine in the fort that the contest was, for them, hopeless; the fight was continued simply as a point of honor. About eleven o'clock General Drayton carried Captain Read's artillery company to the assistance of the men in the fort, who, from excessive labor for several days and during the action, were greatly exhausted. Between twelve and one o'clock Colonel Wagner, commanding the fort, was disabled by a fragment of a shell, and was succeeded by Major Huger. Soon after one o'clock but three guns were in serviceable condition on the water-front, and the ammunition was nearly exhausted. The order was given to stop the hopeless struggle and abandon the fort. Captain Harmes, with three gun detachments, was left to maintain a show of resistance by a slow fire from the three serviceable guns, while the wounded were carried to the rear. The garrison then abandoned the fort, gained their supports, and the whole, including Colonel W. H. Stiles' Georgia Regiment, which had just arrived, retreated hastily from the island. The flight of the garrison was seen and reported "from the tops," when the flag-officer dispatched Commander John Rodgers on shore with a flag of truce. Rodgers, finding that the fort had been abandoned, at 2:20 hoisted the Union flag on the deserted fort. A little later Commander C. H. P. Rodgers was ordered ashore with a detachment of seamen and marines, and took possession of the work.

General Sherman and his corps from their transports were spectators of the action, in which they took no part. A great part of the General's means for disembarking his command had been lost during the storm at sea. When the action was over the troops commenced landing, and the fort was turned over by Commander Rodgers to General H. G. Wright, whose brigade was the first to disembark. No attempt was made to pursue the retreating Confederates, who did not leave the island at Ferry Point on Skull Creek until half-past one o'clock the next morning. Flag-officer Tattnall's steamboats,

after aiding in ferrying the troops across Skull
Creek, proceeded to Savannah by the inland passage.

Comparatively little attention had been given by
the fleet to Fort Beauregard. It was an easy prey
after Fort Walker was taken. The inability of the
forts to protect the harbor against the fleet had been
made manifest, and any attempt longer to hold Bay
Point would not only have been futile, but in all
probability would have resulted in the capture of
the whole force on the island. Colonel Donovant
therefore ordered Captain Elliott to evacuate the
fort, and all of the troops on the island retreated
during the afternoon and night to Beaufort, by a
narrow trail known to but few, across Edding's
Island, which is little more than an impenetrable
marsh. Nothing but what the men carried on their
persons could be taken over such a trail. The retreat was effected without the knowledge of the
enemy, or it might have been cut off by gunboats
passing up Beaufort River and Station Creek to
Jenkins' Landing and White Hall Ferry. The Confederate loss on Hilton Head was eleven killed and
thirty-five seriously wounded, and in Fort Beauregard Captain Elliott and twelve men were badly
wounded. In the fleet eight were killed and twenty-
three wounded.

General Sherman completed the disembarkation
of his corps on the 8th, the greater part landing on
Hilton Head, where the construction of an extensive
intrenched camp was commenced and pressed forward rapidly to completion. Engineer officers made
reconnoissances of the island for the location of such

defensive works as might be needed to make it a secure base of operations. At Braddock's Point, on the southern extremity of the island, one 10-inch gun, two 5½-inch rifles, and two 12-pounder howitzers were found, which were designed for a battery in the course of construction at that point.

CHAPTER IV

If evidence were needed to show that the States
which first withdrew from the Union did not con-
template a war of coercion as one of the first conse-
quences of secession, none more conclusive could be
presented than the defenseless condition of those
States when the war commenced. For it is inconceiv-
able that intelligent men charged with the conduct
of public affairs would have plunged their States, so
unprepared, into so unequal a war. However well
assured they may have been of the right of a State
to withdraw from the Union, or however strong may
have been their convictions that separation from the
Northern States would contribute greatly to the
prosperity and happiness of their own States, they
would surely have deferred the practical assertion
of the right of secession until they had made some
adequate preparation for the maintenance of their
independence. They had no navy, and no means of
building up one of sufficient strength in time to be of
any avail in the defense of hundreds of miles of seacoast—a seacoast which was undefended by forts

and therefore was thus at the mercy of a hostile naval power.

The occupation of Port Royal by the land and naval forces of the United States was a fatal blow to the domestic and social institutions and life of that section of country. It at once reduced the planters of that region from affluence to poverty, a sudden reverse of fortune for which their easy and luxurious mode of life for generations had peculiarly unfitted them.

For many miles inland the South Atlantic coast is penetrated and intersected by innumerable bays, tortuous rivers, creeks, and bayous, which were navigable by steamers of considerable capacity and draft. The arable land of the islands formed by those water-courses is very fertile, producing various crops in abundance, especially the finest sea island cotton in the world. These lands were generally owned in large plantations by gentlemen to whom they had descended from father to son for several generations, and were cultivated by negroes who had been inherited with the land on which they lived.

Probably no class of people ever lived in greater luxury and ease than the proprietors of the sea islands and adjoining plantations on the mainland. The waters teemed with shell and other fish in great variety and excellence, and in season were covered with innumerable water fowl. Deer, wild turkeys, and other game were abundant on the islands, and all requisites for comfortable and luxurious living which the land and water did not produce in kind were procurable from the proceeds of the cultivated crops. The commodious residences of the planters were generally surrounded by extensive grounds, shaded by stately oaks, magnolias, and other forest trees gracefully festooned with the long gray hanging moss, and adorned by a lavish wealth of vines, shrubs, and flowers which in that mild climate grow in a profuse luxuriance unknown in colder regions. Many of the houses were models of comfort and luxury, adorned with works of art and well-selected libraries,—and served by retinues of well-trained servants—in all respects suitable residences for the refined and cultivated proprietors, generally educated gentlemen who divided their time between the management of their estates and the direction of political affairs, enlivened by field sports and in dispensing the generous hospitality which was characteristic of their order.

The occupation of Port Royal exposed the whole of the region of country to the invaders, whose gunboats and transports could penetrate through all the ramifications of the watercourses to the very doors of planters' residences. The planters and their sons capable of bearing arms were generally in the army, their wives and children residing on their estates in the accustomed confident security, surrounded by the numerous plantation and house servants, fearing nothing from them while their moral influence and restraint remained undisturbed. The appearance of the Union gunboats produced the wildest panic in those communities—homes were hastily abandoned by their white inhabitants, the women, flying from perils worse to them than death, left their luxurious homes to the pillage of bands of demoralized negroes.

The day after landing at Hilton Head General Sherman reports to the Adjutant General: "The effect of this victory is startling. Every white inhabitant has left the island. The wealthy islands of Saint Helena, Ladies' and most of Port Royal are abandoned by the whites, and the beautiful estates of the planters, with all their immense property, left to the pillage of hordes of apparently disaffected blacks, and the indications are that the panic has extended to the fort on the north end of Reynolds' Island commanding the fine anchorage of Saint Helena Sound."

The "hordes of blacks" had not a monopoly of the pillage of the "immense property left on the fine estates"; opportunities and temptations to pillage were too many and strong to be resisted. They recall the temptation that beset the early British conquerors of Bengal when the victory of Plassey placed the untold treasures of Moorshedabad at their disposal; and Lord Clive's famous exclamation when defending himself in the House of Commons for the share he received of the treasures of that magnificent capital, "By God, Mr. Chairman, at this moment I stand astonished at my own moderation." In a short time there was little of value left on those plantations.

Three days after landing General Sherman was constrained to issue a general order rebuking some of his officers and men for their active participation in the pillage, and instructing his brigade and other commanding officers to suppress all such depredations.

About fifteen miles above Bay Point was the beautiful town of Beaufort—a town of private residences belonging to the wealthiest planters on the islands. The town was noted for the beauty and elegance of its private residences and grounds, and nowhere in South Carolina, or in any other State, was there a more refined, cultivated, and hospitable community. On the 8th the gunboats *Seneca, Penguin,* and *Pembina* steamed cautiously up Beaufort River, with orders from Flag-officer DuPont, if fired on from batteries, as it was supposed they would be, to retire out of range and notify the flag-officer, that a proper force might be sent to reduce the works. But there were no batteries on the river-banks, and when the gunboats came in sight of the town a few horsemen were seen riding away. There was not a white person in the town, which swarmed with negroes frantically plundering the luxurious residences and carrying away their costly booty in every boat or other conveyance they could lay their hands on.

The negroes left on the islands soon became objects of solicitude and embarrassment to the Union general commanding. They dearly loved and luxuriated in idleness, and when freed from the control and direction of their masters freely indulged their natural propensity. Comparatively few of them came into the military posts, and to the surprise of the industrious and thrifty troops from New England, they manifested little inclination to work regularly for wages. So long as they could procure food they preferred to remain in idleness at their old and often devastated homes. Many of those who came into the posts and engaged to work, tired of it and escaped back to their old haunts. Proverbially improvident and accustomed all their lives to being cared for and supplied with the necessaries of life by their masters, they naturally looked to the white people who had come among them for food and clothing. Common humanity required that they should not be allowed to starve, and it was plain that they would soon be a heavy tax on the commissary and quartermaster's departments. To relieve the Government of such a burden and make the negroes self-sustaining, General Sherman divided the part of the country under his control into districts of convenient size for efficient supervision, over each of which he purposed to appoint an agent or overseer to organize the negroes and direct them in working the plantations. All of the horses and mules having been carried off, and most of them appropriated to the use of the United States Government, it was necessary to procure others, and the Secretary of the Treasury, having regard to the interest of the government in the cultivation of cotton, called on the Secretary of War to furnish the necessary teams.

While the land forces were engaged in short reconnoissances of Hilton Head and other neighboring islands, and making themselves secure and comfortable in their newly acquired positions, most of the naval vessels were sent to the various blockading

stations, and the lighter draft gunboats were sent off
to reconnoiter the country bordering the inland navigable waters up and down the coast. Commander
Percival Drayton, a native of that part of the
country, went northward toward Charleston in the
Pawnee, accompanied by the *Pembina* and the
steamer *Vixen* of the Coast Survey. His knowledge
of the country well fitted him for the duty, and he
was accompanied by Captain Boutelle, whose long
service in that quarter on coast survey duty had
given him accurate knowledge of the watercourses
and the positions of the residences of planters, where
he had often been a welcome guest. On Otter Island
at the entrance to Saint Helena Sound they found a
deserted field-work. This was deemed an important
point, and Flag-officer DuPont undertook to guard
it until some of the land forces could occupy it.
Going up the Coosaw River another abandoned
field-work was found near the mouth of Bamwell
Creek. Ascending the Ashepoo about four miles,
another abandoned earthwork was found. A little
later the same commander ascended the last mentioned river to the mouth of Mosquito Creek, where
the inland navigation to Charleston commences, and
landing on Hutchinson Island found that the barns
and other outhouses had been burned by the owners
on the approach of the gunboats. No white person
—only some negroes—were found on the island.

Extending his reconnoissance, he went into North
Edisto. Quite an extensive line of abandoned earthworks was found on Edisto Island. Learning from
some negroes that there was a Confederate camp

at Rockville, a pretty village on a river bluff on Wadmalaw Island, a few miles from Edisto, Commander Drayton approached in the *Vixen,* followed by the gunboats. The camp was occupied by a battalion of 292 men, of Colonel John L. Branch's Rifle Regiment, Colonel Branch commanding. On the approach of the gunboats Colonel Branch withdrew his battalion beyond range. Fifty marines and sailors were landed at the wharf, where there was no sign of life. The camp, which was about a mile distant, had been abandoned, Colonel Branch apprehending that if he did not withdraw his command it would be cut off from escape to Johns' Island, and captured.

Commander John Rodgers in the *Flag,* accompanied by the *Seneca* and *Pocahontas,* reconnoitered Tybee Island at the mouth of the Savannah, and receiving no reply to his fire on the earthworks, discovered that they, too, had been dismantled and abandoned. This point also that flag-officer deemed of sufficient importance to be held by the navy until General Sherman could find it convenient to occupy the island with a part of his troops.

Commander C. R. P. Rodgers examined Warsaw Sound, Wilmington River, Ossabaw, Ogeechee, and Vernon rivers. A fort on Warsaw Island was found to have been dismantled and abandoned. A few miles up Wilmington River an occupied work was found, and another on Green Island, commanding Vernon River, the Little Ogeechee, Hell Gate, and the passage from Vernon River into the Great Ogeechee. This fort indicated that it was occupied, by throwing a couple of shells at very long range at the gunboats, the first sign of opposition they had encountered since the bombardment of Forts Walker and Beauregard.

Before Christmas the inland waters had been examined by the navy from the Stono to Ossabaw Sound, and the only occupied works were at those extreme points of that line of coast. The plantations visited presented pictures of destruction and desolation. The appearance of Commander Drayton's boats in the vicinity of a plantation was generally a signal to the master or his agent to apply the torch to his cotton houses, to prevent that valuable crop from falling into the hands of the enemy. The reconnoisances were made in the latter part of November and late into December. If they had been made earlier the armaments of some of the abandoned works might have fallen into their hands.

When it was known in Richmond that the fleet and expeditionary corps had arrived at Port Royal, an order issued from the War Department, November 5, constituting the coast of South Carolina, Georgia, and Florida a military department, and assigning General Lee to the command. That officer hastened to his new field of duty and assumed command under most discouraging circumstances. He went immediately to Coosawhatchie, the nearest point on the Charleston & Savannah Railroad to Port Royal Ferry, and on the afternoon of the 7th, while riding to Hilton Head, met General Ripley and learned from him that the Confederate troops were retreating from Forts Walker and Beauregard and the enemy in complete possession of that the finest harbor on the coast. It was plain that possession of that important harbor gave the enemy control of the inland navigation and all of the islands on the coast, and most seriously threatened both Charleston and Savannah. His sloops-of-war and large steamers could ascend Broad River to Mackay's Point, the mouth of the Pocotaligo, less than ten miles from the Charleston & Savannah Railroad; his gunboats could ascend some miles up both the Coosawhatchie and Pocotaligo rivers, and smaller boats could ascend still further toward the road. There were no guns in position to resist the powerful naval batteries, and there was no recourse left to General Lee but to prepare to meet the enemy in the field, and if the enemy should move forward with the promptness and vigor which the number and capacity of the war vessels and transports then in Port Royal harbor indicated he was capable of throwing into his campaign, the prospects of meeting him successfully in the field were exceedingly discouraging.

On retreating from Hilton Head General Thomas F. Drayton halted his command of less than a thousand men at Bluffton, about eleven miles from Fort Walker. The Georgia troops which had joined him the day before continued on to Savannah. Colonel Donovant, after crossing his command of six or seven hundred men to the mainland at Port Royal Ferry, was halted at Garden's Corner, a mile or so on the road to Pocotaligo. Neither of these commands had brought anything with them except their arms from the islands, and were in very destitute condition. Colonel Clingman's regiment of North Carolina volunteers, six companies of Colonel Edwards' infantry, and Colonel Martin's cavalry regiment,—the two last of South Carolina volunteers,— were at and near Coosawhatchie. There was no field artillery. The whole force from Charleston to the Savannah River was less than four thousand men. On November 19, two weeks after the Union forces had arrived in Port Royal harbor, the Governor of South Carolina reported to General Lee that there were 13,100 South Carolina troops in the State. That was probably the number down on the rolls, and small as it was greatly exceeded the numbers present for duty. That force was distributed from Georgetown to Hardeeville, S. C., a distance of about 175 miles. Over about half of the distance only was there railroad communication. A large proportion of this force was necessarily held in the works for the defense of Charleston.

On November 10 General A. R. Lawton, commanding in Georgia, reported to General Lee that he had only about 5500 troops, 2000 of them under General Mercer, near Brunswick. The remainder were between the Altamaha and Savannah, and all but 500 of them within twenty miles of the latter city. Of his whole force but 500 were cavalry, and there were but three field batteries, very scantily supplied with horses.

As late as December 24 General Lee, writing to Judge Magrath, President of the State Convention (about to assemble), in regard to the preparations for the defense of the State, says: "I have not been able to get an accurate report of the troops under my command in the State. I hope it may be as large as you state, but I am sure those for duty fall far short of it. For instance, DeSaussure's brigade is put down at 3420 men. When last in Charleston (the day I inquired) I was informed that in one regiment there were 110 men for duty in camp on the race course, and in the other about 200. Colonel Branch, I am told, had only about 200 men with him at Rockville, though I have had no official report of his retreat from there. The companies of mounted men in the service are very much reduced. The Charleston Light Dragoons and Rutledge Mounted Rifles have about 45 men each. The companies of Colonel Martin's regiment are very small. One of them, Captain Fripp's, reports 4 commissioned officers and 19 privates. It is very expensive to retain in service companies of such strength, and I think all had better be reorganized. I have only on this line [the letter was written at his headquarters at Coosawhatchie] for field operations Heyward's, DeSaussure's, Dunovant's, Jones', and Edwards' regiments from South Carolina and Martin's cavalry. General Ripley writes that Elford's and Means' regiments are poorly armed and equipped, and at present ineffective, and that the organization of the troops thrown forward on James Island is so brittle that he fears it will break. The garrisons at Moultrie, Sumter, Johnson, and the fixed batteries— the best and most stable of our forces—cannot be removed from them; neither can those at Georgetown, and should not be counted among those for operations in the field. You must not understand that this is written in a complaining spirit. I know the difficulties in the way, and wish you to understand them, explain them to the Governor, and, if possible, remove them. Our enemy increases in strength faster than we do. Where he will strike I do not know, but the blow, when it does fall, will be hard."

To General Ripley he writes: "Unless more field artillery can be obtained, it will be almost impossible to make head against the enemy should he land in any force."

The scarcity of arms which existed from the beginning to the close of the war was manifested by the urgent and repeated appeals of the Governors of South Carolina, Georgia, and Florida to General Lee, the Secretary of War and the President, for ten thousand Enfield rifles brought by the blockade runner *Fingal*, Major Anderson commanding, which succeeded in running into Savannah on November 13.

CHAPTER V

At Port Royal—a central position as regards this
long and insecurely guarded Confederate line—
General Sherman had in hand a compact and thoroughly equipped body of about 13,000 men, and
there was present, besides, a fine battalion of 600
marines. The co-operating fleet in the harbor could
cover a landing within five or six miles of Coosawhatchie, or at almost any other desirable point on
the coast. Luckily,—or unluckily as it may be regarded,—for the Confederates the Union general
seems to have regarded his position as one in which
it behooved him to move with great deliberation and
caution.

After inspecting the batteries and posts from
Charleston to Fernandina, Fla., General Lee directed
all guns to be withdrawn from the less important
points and employed in the defense of Charleston,
Savannah, and the entrance to Cumberland Sound
and Brunswick, Ga. The attempt to hold the entrance to Cumberland Sound was soon abandoned,

and the general's plan of defense was restricted to holding the two most important points, Charleston and Savannah, the line of the railroad between those two cities, and the country between it and the sea islands. Other points, such as Georgetown, S. C., Fernandina, Jacksonville, and Saint Augustine were held, but not in force or with any expectation of successfully defending them against a formidable and persistent attack. For the better administration of his extensive department, the coast of South Carolina was divided into five military districts, as follows:

The First, extending from Little River Inlet to South Santee River, under command of Colonel Arthur Middleton Manigault; headquarters, Georgetown.

The Second, from the South Santee to the Stono River and up Rantowles Creek, embracing Charleston and its harbor, under command of Brigadier General Roswell S. Ripley; headquarters, Charleston.

The Third composed the country between the Stono and Ashepoo rivers, under command of Brigadier General N. G. Evans; headquarters, Adams Run.

The Fourth extended from the Ashepoo to Port Royal entrance, thence through Colliton River and Ocala Creek, Ferebeville, under command of Brigadier General John C. Pemberton; headquarters, Coosawhatchie.

The Fifth embraced the country between the last named boundary and the Savannah River, under command of Brigadier General Thomas F. Drayton; headquarters, Hardeeville.

Brigadier General A. R. Lawton remained in command in Georgia, and Brigadier General James H. Trapier commanded in middle and east Georgia. On Generals Lawton and Ripley devolved the responsibility of defending Savannah and Charleston, and under direction of the department commander they pushed forward the several defensive works with all possible haste.

The field for military operations opened to General Sherman was so extensive and its possibilities so many that he seems to have been bewildered. He could not decide definitely at what point to strike, and his perplexity was heightened by the exaggerated reports he received, and believed, of the number of troops he would have to encounter whenever he should move against the enemy. Thus he writes in November that the main body of the Confederate force was at Pocotaligo, another large body collecting at Grahamville, and still others between the latter place and the Savannah River, with their advance post at Bluffton, whereas, as has been stated, there were not more than 4000 troops between Charleston and the Savannah River; again that his latest news confirmed what he had previously ascertained, that there were 20,000 troops in and about Savannah, among them two regiments of cavalry and four field batteries; and later he writes to General McClellan that he had information that there were "about 65,000 in and about that city, which is well fortified both on the land and river sides. They

are moving heaven and earth for a secure defense."
His own judgment was that upon the whole it would
be best to attack and capture Savannah. Reconnoissances made by engineer officers had early developed the fact that it was practicable to pass gunboats by inland navigation into the Savannah River
by the left bank at two points, one being two, and the
other six miles above Fort Pulaski, and that the
river might also be entered above the fort from the
south by Wilmington River and St. Augustine
Creek. General Sherman desired to utilize these
inland passages to move a combined land and naval
force up the river and take the city by a coup-de-
main. Admiral DuPont was, however, unwilling to
risk his gunboats through the intricate passages into
the river without a more thorough examination.
Then the General proposed to capture the city by
siege, if necessary, but before he could make any
aggressive move he needed additional troops and
transportation. First he asked for a regiment of
cavalry, one of regular artillery, ten regiments of
infantry, and a pontoon train; and later asked for
twenty regiments of infantry. Reinforcements were
sent to him from time to time, until at the end of
February he had an aggregate force present of
17,875 men. The most favorable season for operations in that locality passed, however, without any
important move, and in the meantime the Confederates profited by the delay to strengthen their lines
and increase their force. Every day's delay made
the capture of Savannah more difficult, until General McClellan, general-in-chief of the army, wrote

to General Sherman discouraging a siege of the
city, and advising that the preparations for the
reduction of Fort Pulaski be pushed forward to
completion.

"I am forced to the conclusion," he says, "that
under present circumstances the siege and capture
of Savannah do not promise results commensurate
with the sacrifices necessary. I do not consider the
possession of Savannah worth a siege after Pulaski
is in our hands. But the possession of Pulaski is of
the first importance. But, after all, the greatest
moral effect would be produced by the reduction of
Charleston and its defenses. There the rebellion
had its birth; there the unnatural hatred of our
Government is most intense; there is the center of
the boasted power and courage of the rebels."

The capture and occupation of Fernandina, Fla.,
had long been one of the purposes which the Expeditionary Corps should accomplish, but had been
delayed from time to time awaiting, it would seem,
naval co-operation. About March 1 Brigadier
General H. G. Wright's brigade sailed for that
place, accompanied by Admiral DuPont and his
fleet. In the meantime the capture of Fort Donelson
and retreat southward of General A. S. Johnston's
army made it necessary to reinforce him with troops
from other departments, among them the Department of South Carolina, Georgia, and Florida,
which obliged General Lee to contract his lines. He
had therefore ordered Fort Clinch and other batteries on Amelia Island to be dismantled and abandoned. In consequence General Wright took pos-

session of Fernandina without opposition. In a
few days the fleet proceeded up the St. Johns River
and near the end of the month was followed by
General Wright, who occupied Jacksonville and St.
Augustine, which had also been abandoned. Hence
by the end of March the Union troops held the important points on the coast from North Edisto Inlet
to St. Augustine, a distance of about 250 miles, and
with the exception of the bombardment of the works
in Port Royal Harbor, all of these points had been
occupied without opposition.

Early in December Captain Q. A. Gillmore,
chief engineer on General Sherman's staff, having
made under instructions an examination of Tybee
Island and Fort Pulaski for the purpose of ascertaining the practicability of reducing the fort, reported it practicable, and submitted a plan of operations. His plan, with some slight modifications,
was approved both by his chief and the War Department, and preparations were promptly commenced for carrying it into execution. As a preliminary step the Forty-sixth New York Regiment
of Volunteers, Colonel R. Rosa, commanding, was
sent to occupy Big Tybee Island.

Fort Pulaski was built on Cockspur Island, Ga.,
at the head of Tybee Roads, and commanded both
channels of the Savannah River. The island was
simply a deposit of mud about a mile long and half
mile wide, and was about fourteen miles from Savannah.

The river is but little if any more than an average
of a mile and a quarter in width and between the

fort and city are several islands similar in formation to Cockspur, stretching in the direction of the current. The first and most obvious step in proceeding to reduce the fort was to cut it off from the city by batteries, to be erected on the banks or the middle islands. But the islands and banks,—if deposits of soft mud scarcely above the water level at ordinary high tide, and submerged by high spring tides or when the wind is in a certain quarter, may be called banks,—are exceedingly ill adapted to the construction of batteries. On both sides of the river these deposits of mud extend for many miles and are thickly covered with tall reeds and coarse grass, giving to the country the appearance suggestive of the appropriate name of the river. They are intersected by numerous tortuous bayous, dividing the shore up into islands, making it practicable for passage between the fort and city in small rowboats when the river itself is closed.

Captain Gillmore was given the rank of Brigadier General of Volunteers, and charged with the task of reducing Fort Pulaski.

With incredible labor a battery of six guns (twenty- and thirty-pounder Parrott rifles and an eight-inch siege howitzer) was constructed by troops of General Viele's Brigade, at Venus Point on Jones' Island, about five miles above the fort. The guns and material were carried from Daufuskie Island, four miles distant, the nearest point of firm ground on which troops could camp. The guns were carried in the night by hand about three-fourths of a mile over a marsh of unctuous mud, on a tramway of shifting planks, in which the wheels, when they slipped, would sink to the hubs and the men nearly to the waists. There was a drenching rain during the night, and for the greater part of twenty-four hours the men at work were up to their waists in mud and water. The battery was in condition for service.

Three days later a similar battery was constructed on Birds Island directly opposite Venus Point. Admiral Tattnall's little fleet of river steamers, which had escaped on the morning of February 11 from Port Royal, steamed down the river and engaged the Venus Point battery, but was driven off. Before the end of February two companies of the Forty-sixth New York Volunteers, with a battery of two field pieces and a thirty pounder Parrott gun—stationed first on Decent Island, and subsequently on an old hulk in Lazaretto Creek, about 2¼ miles from Pulaski—and a small gunboat in the same creek, in conjunction with the batteries on Venus Point and Bird Island, effectually isolated Pulaski. It would necessarily have had to surrender through starvation when the supply of provisions should be consumed; nevertheless the work for its bombardment and reduction went on.

It was not until February 21 that the first vessel having the necessary ordnance and ordnance stores and engineering supplies arrived off the entrance to Savannah River. Tybee, like the other islands bordering the lower river, is mainly a deposit of mud, but it is somewhat better adapted to siege operations than the others, in that there are on it a few ridges and hummocks of firm ground, and the shore on Tybee Roads, where it was proposed to construct the batteries, is particularly skirted by low sandbanks. The distance from the landing-place on the island to the most advanced batteries was about 2½ miles, the last mile presenting the same obstacles to the transportation of heavy ordnance as had been encountered and surmounted on Jones Island, and was, besides, within range of Pulaski's guns. A causeway was constructed on fascines and brushwood over the marshy ground, which trembled like jelly under the tramp and mallets of the laborers, and when the thin upper crust was broken through a pole or oar could be thrust ten or twelve feet in the soft mud. The herculean labor of transporting thirty-six of the heaviest guns then in use,— some of them weighting 8½ tons,—with the necessary ammunition and the appliances was performed by the soldiers, nearly all of it in the night, often in thick darkness and drenching rain, regardless of weather and the miasma of the marshes spread out for many miles around them. Two hundred and fifty men could with difficulty drag a single piece.

On the evening of April 9 the batteries were completed and all was in readiness for the bombardment. There were eleven batteries mounting thirty-six guns, viz.: twelve 13-inch and four 10-inch mortars, six 10-inch and four 8-inch columbiads, five 30-pounder Parrott rifles, and five James rifles, 48-, 64-, and 84-pounders. The breaching batteries were at an average distance of 1700 yards from the fort; the four 10-inch siege mortars were 1650

yards distant; the 13-inch mortars at distances varying from 2400 to 3400 yards.

Fort Pulaski, on which these batteries were in
readiness to open, was built of brick; was pentago-
nal in shape and casemated on all sides. Its walls
were 7½ feet thick and in height 25 feet above
high water. It was arranged for one tier of guns
in embrasure and one in barbette. The gorge was
covered by an earthen outwork or demi-lune of bold
relief. The main work and demi-lune were surrounded by wet ditches—the one around the main
work 48 feet and that around the demi-lune 32 feet
wide. Communication with the exterior was through
the gorge, over a drawbridge into the demi-lune,
through a face of which was a passage by another
drawbridge over the ditch of the demi-lune. A full
armament for the fort would have been 140 guns.
At the time of the bombardment it mounted 46
guns, varying in class from 12-pounder howitzers to
10-inch columbiads. Twenty of the heaviest of
the guns bore on the Tybee Island batteries. The
fort was garrisoned by five companies of the First
Georgia Regiment,—aggregate strength 385—Colonel Charles H. Olmstead commanding.

At sunrise on the morning of April 10 a summons
to surrender was sent under flag of truce, Lieutenant
James H. Wilson of the engineers bearing it to Colonel Olmstead. The summons was refused. Fire
was immediately opened, and soon the thirty-six
guns on Tybee and those of the fort which could be
brought to bear on them were in full and active
play. The bombardment continued without inter-

ruption for 10½ hours, and till it was too dark to see distinctly. It then ceased. Throughout the night two heavy mortars and a 30-pounder Parrott maintained a slow fire, throwing a shell about every five minutes, to interrupt any repairs that might be attempted. At sunrise on the 11th the bombardment was renewed, with greater accuracy than on the previous day. The breach which had commenced under the first day's fire rapidly extended, and by 12 M. two casemates had been battered wide open. A third was rapidly crumbling under the concentrated fire when, at 2 P. M., the white flag was run up over the fort, which, with its armament and garrison, was surrendered to the Union forces.

The reduction of Pulaski reflected great credit on the officers and men engaged, especially on General Gillmore, under whose personal direction it was commenced and continued to a successful issue. The troops who participated in all of the heavy labor of the preparation and bombardment were the Seventh Connecticut Volunteer Infanry, Colonel Alfred H. Terry, commanding; the Forty-sixth New York, Colonel Randolph Rosa; two companies of the New York Engineers, Lieutenant Colonel James F. Hall; two companies of the Third Rhode Island Artillery, and a small detachment of engineer troops of the regular army.

It is worthy of note as illustrative of the readiness with which the volunteers adapted themselves to any service demanded of them, that with the exception of a detachment of sailors from the frigate *Wabash*, who served four light siege guns the

second day, the labor of mounting and serving the
guns was performed by men who had no experience
whatever as artillerists. They were directed by
well-trained officers.

In the reduction of Fort Pulaski the superior
capacity of rifled cannon over smooth bores was
very clearly exemplified, and marks a new era in
siege operations. Up to that time from five hundred to seven hundred yards was regarded as the
extreme distances at which an exposed wall of a
well-constructed fort could be breached. By the
use of fifty-eight per cent. only of rifled guns a wide
and practicable breach was made in the walls of
Pulaski, under 18 hours of continuous fire, at an
average distance of 1700 yards.

Extensive as was the territory over which the
combined land and naval forces under General Sherman and Admiral DuPont had hoisted the Union
flag, the editors of the most influential Northern
papers had not been slow to discover that all had
not been accomplished which might, in their judg-
ments, have been expected and demanded of so
large a force fitted out and maintained at such vast
cost to the Government. Adverse criticism had
commenced early, and continued until a change was
effected in the command of the land force. General Sherman, under whose command the reduction
of Fort Pulaski had been planned and pressed forward under great difficulties to within a few days
of its actual accomplishment, was not permitted to
witness the only triumph in arms of his corps, and
receive the surrender of the fort. On March 15

an order from the War Department in Washington created a new military department, composed of the States of South Carolina, Georgia, and Florida, designated as the Department of the South, and Major General David Hunter was assigned to the command. Brigadier General H. W. Benham was assigned to the command of the troops of the Expeditionary Corps, designated as the Northern Division of the Department of the South. General Hunter assumed command on March 31, and was on Tybee Island in time to demand the surrender of Fort Pulaski, and report its reduction to his Government.

On March 2 President Davis had called General Lee to Richmond, and Major General John C. Pemberton succeeded him in command.

CHAPTER VI

Cotton being the basis of financial credit of the Southern Confederacy, it was manifestly of the first importance that the government should hold some seaports from which the cotton could be shipped and into which the return cargoes could be entered. Charleston and Savannah were the most important ports of entry on the South Atlantic coast. These two cities were connected by a railroad of about one hundred and fifteen miles in length, lying broadside to the coast, which is intersected by numerous bays, inlets, rivers, and creeks, forming a network of watercourses navigable to within easy striking distance of this railroad at several points.

Before the close of the first year of the war the Federal land and naval forces were in secure possession of important points on the coast of South Carolina and of the navigable waters that border it and extend far into the interior. Wherever their fleets could be brought the Confederates could offer no effective opposition to the landing of troops, except at points within range of fixed batteries, which at that early period of the war were few and very incomplete. The Confederates had nothing to oppose effectively to the heavy guns of the Federal fleet, which could sweep over the low banks of the rivers of that country with irresistible force. Skillful engineers had selected with admirable judgment the most important and vital points for the defense of the cities and the coast generally, and the construction of the necessary earthworks under the direction and superintendence of competent engineers was a mere question of tools and manual labor. But the arming of the works when constructed with suitable guns and ammunition was a far more difficult task.

The Confederacy labored under far greater difficulties as to the supply of suitable arms and ammunition than is generally supposed. While some of the guns, both of heavy ordnance and small arms, that were found in the forts and arsenals within the limits of the Confederacy were among the best then known to the military profession in this country, much the greater part of them were of old and antiquated pattern, and even the best of them were soon rendered comparatively ineffective when opposed to the new and improved arms of all kinds that the exigencies of the war and the inventive genius of the country soon supplied and brought into use. There were no great manufactories of arms, ammunition, and the various munitions of war in the Confederacy. The South was essentially an agricultural country, and manufacturing generally formed but a small part of its productive industry. The manufacture of arms, gunpowder, and the various munitions of war generally were especially but little practiced or known; and the rigid blockade of the Southern coast, which was soon established and maintained, while it by no means sealed the Southern ports, greatly obstructed the introduction into the country of all manner of arms and munitions of war and the materials necessary for their manufacture.

In the beginning the Confederate Government selected a most accomplished and efficient officer as the head of the Ordnance Department in the person of the late General J. Gorgas, who may be said to have inaugurated new industries in the country, all directed to the production of arms and their various accessories absolutely essential to the prosecution of war. With efficient aids, such as General George W. Raines and Major Garesché, who established powder mills, and Captain Brook, who introduced an admirable rifled cannon (which bore his name), and others in other branches, he very soon had the Ordnance Department in wonderfully successful and efficient operation.

But in the first year of the war the government was wholly unable to supply suitable siege, garrison, and field guns for the various forts and batteries or small arms to put into the hands of the volunteers. Hence it was that all along the coast and in the interior Confederate artillerists manned and used many antiquated guns, mounted on clumsy carriages, and in the field Southern infantry and cavalry, armed with old-pattern muskets, sometimes with flint-locks, shot-guns, sporting rifles, and pistols, encountered foemen armed with the best weapons of modern warfare. And while new and improved arms were constantly introduced in the North, this inferiority of armament continued in the South throughout the war.[1] Generally the best arms in the Confederate army were gathered on the battlefield. It is not probable that much use was made in the Federal army of the Confederate arms gathered in the same way.

With land forces securely established on the coast and the navy in undisputed possession of the sea, and with ample transportation at command, the Federal commanders on the Southern coast possessed a base of operations which threatened at once Charleston on their right, Savannah on the left, and the connecting railroad and intermediate country. The Confederate authorities very naturally apprehended that so soon as the Federal forces were thus in possession of the coast the commanders would avail themselves of their resources to seize upon the

[1]General La Grange, a distinguished Federal cavalry commander, recently told the writer that in the winter campaign in east Tennessee of 1863-64 it seemed to him almost unfair and cruel to meet in battle with Spencer repeating rifles Confederates generally armed with muzzle-loading arms, one of the former being equivalent in a fight to six or eight of the latter.

Charleston & Savannah Railroad near the head of Broad River, sever the connection between those two cities, and with the combined land and naval forces envelop alternately each of those important places. That, it was plainly seen, would be a combination difficult to resist successfully.

The capture of Charleston especially would have been disastrous to the Confederacy in every point of view—commercial, military, and political. The city would not only have been lost as a shipping port, but the railroad communication with Virginia, North Carolina, and eastern Georgia would have been cut off and the upper roads by Branchville would have been placed in jeopardy by the presence of a hostile force so near as Charleston. It is fair, too, to presume that the capture of Charleston would have caused as general satisfaction throughout the North as the capture of Richmond, and the political effect would have been as encouraging and stimulating there as it would have been depressing and discouraging in the South. Yet notwithstanding the importance of the two cities mentioned, and their connecting railroads, their vulnerability and the ample resources both on land and sea at the command of the Federal Government, they were defended and firmly held for nearly four years against every attack made against them, and were only abandoned when the march of the great army under General Sherman from the west to the sea rendered them no longer tenable. It is proposed to sketch here only the principal operations against Charleston and to tell how they were met and brought to naught.

In the spring of 1862 Major General David Hunter, United States Army, commanded the Department of the South, with headquarters at Hilton Head, and Admiral DuPont commanded the South Atlantic Squadron. Major General John C. Pemberton, Confederate States Army, commanded the Department of South Carolina and Georgia, headquarters in Charleston. Soon after the capture of Fort Pulaski Brigadier General H. W. Benham, commanding a division and second in rank to General Hunter, submitted to the latter and to Admiral DuPont a plan for the capture of Charleston. Though favorably considered, it was not at once adopted. On April 28 Admiral DuPont sent to General Hunter reports from Captains Marchand and Mullany, of the navy, giving information, which they had derived from sources deemed reliable, as to the force present for the defense of Charleston. The information was to the effect that the force in Charleston and within ten miles of it was from 2650 to 2860. Of this force between 1500 and 1600 were on James Island, between the mouth of the Stono and Charleston, and about 600 at Fort Johnson.

About the middle of May a crew of negroes, who escaped from Charleston with the steamer *Planter,* carried to Hilton Head the additional news that the Confederate troops and guns had withdrawn from Coles' and Battery islands, thus leaving the entrance to the Stono unguarded. Gunboats sent by Admiral DuPont to reconnoiter entered the river without opposition, and Captain Percival Drayton re-

ported to the Admiral: "We are in as complete possession of the river [Stono] as of Port Royal and
can land and protect the army whenever it wants."
Finding this gateway to Charleston thrown wide
open, General Hunter decided to adopt General Benham's plan and make a dash to take the city by a
coup-de-main. Preparations to carry the plan into
execution were pressed forward rapidly.

James Island was generally regarded as the key
to Charleston. It was the opinion of the most competent military engineers that if the Union army
could once secure footing on that island the fall of
Charleston would be inevitable and only a question
of time. The plan of attack, briefly stated, was to
land a force of 10,000 men of all arms on the lower
end of James Island and by rapid movement overtake, engage, and defeat the Confederate force on
the island before it could be reinforced. That accomplished, a securely entrenched camp would be
established beyond the range of the guns of Fort
Sumter and in easy shelling range of the city. From
that position, strengthened by reinforcements which
were expected, it would require a much larger force
to dislodge them than the Confederate Government
could assemble while all of the available force in
the eastern States of the Confederacy was in front
of Richmond, to meet General McClellan, then
marching on that city, and in Mississippi, confronting General Halleck. All these conditions of the
military problem seemed favorable for the success of
the proposed plan of operations.

This plan embraced, first, a preliminary expedition to cut the Charleston & Savannah Railroad and destroy it from Salkehatchie to Coosawhatchie, a precautionary measure to prevent the passage of reinforcements from the latter to the former city. Brigadier General I. J. Stephens, who commanded a division at Beaufort, was directed to execute that part of the plan. General Stephens ordered Colonel B. C. Christ, of the Fiftieth Pennsylvania Infantry, to take his own regiment, one company each of the Eighth Michigan and Seventy-ninth New York Highlanders, a battalion of the First Massachusetts Cavalry and one section of Rockwell's light battery of Connecticut Artillery, in all about nine hundred men, and to proceed to the execution of the plan. This force crossed at Port Royal Ferry in the night of May 28, was on the mainland by daylight the next morning, and marched immediately for Pocotaligo, via Garden's Corner and the Shelden Road, and was considerably delayed, says Colonel Christ, by the Confederate pickets before reaching Old Pocotaligo, about ten miles from Port Royal Ferry. General Stephens regarded the force under Colonel Christ as ample for the accomplishment of the object of the expedition; nevertheless, "out of abundant caution," he sent the Eighth Michigan and Seventy-ninth Highlanders to Garden's Corner and the One Hundredth Pennsylvania to the Ferry as reserves.

The approach to Old Pocotaligo by the road the Federal troops were marching is over a causeway partly flanked on either side by a marsh, through which runs a narrow stream, spanned by a bridge about fifteen feet in length. The flooring of the bridge had been torn off, leaving the string-pieces. The marsh was bordered by a skirt of woods. In the woods, and partly sheltered by the banks of ditches, were parts of three companies of Confederate cavalry, viz.: Captain Trenholm's company of the Rutledge Mounted Rifles and Companies A and D of the First Battalion South Carolina Cavalry. Some were armed with rifles, others with shotguns. They were all dismounted and numbered only 76 men. Their horses were about half a mile in the rear, where the other two companies of the First Battalion and Captain D. B. Haywood's company were held in reserve. Many of these men were armed only with sabers. They numbered in all 110 and were commanded by Major I. H. Morgan. Colonel W. S. Walker commanded the whole.

At this point the Federal advance was disputed; the seventy-six dismounted cavalrymen held their position with admirable tenacity, keeping the enemy at bay for more than two hours and a half, from half-past ten until after one o'clock, and until Captain Parker, of the Fiftieth Pennsylvania, passed over the bridge at the head of his company and was followed by the remaining companies, which, deploying to the right and left of the road, flanked the Confederates, obliging them to fall back to their support, which they did in good order and with little loss. In this affair the gallant Captain Parker was killed. The bridge was so repaired as to enable the cavalry and artillery to pass, and Colonel Christ and his command pressed forward in pursuit and continued to advance until they came in full view and within a quarter of a mile of the railroad the destruction of which was the object of the expedition.

In the meantime the artillery had come up with the infantry and cavalry, not in time, however, to take part in the affair at Old Pocotaligo, because the officer in command, Lieutenant Cannon, had halted two hours on the march to feed and water his horses. But the weather was warm, the men were fatigued and had expended nearly all of their ammunition. Some negroes had told Colonel Christ that "the desperate stand by the enemy" at Old Pocotaligo was made because they confidently looked for reinforcements. As the Colonel says:

"In view of the positive orders I received to return to Port Royal Island during the night, and to avoid, if possible, bringing on a general engagement with reduced ammunition, I deemed it prudent to retire, and accordingly arrived at Port Royal Ferry at 11 o'clock P. M."

Colonel Walker, having been reinforced by two companies of infantry and three pieces of field artillery, under Captain Stephen Elliott, followed in pursuit to Garden's Corner, where a few shots were exchanged. The night was too intensely dark to attack, and when morning dawned the Federal force had crossed the ferry and was out of reach. General Stephens says:

"In short, the operation was most successful as a reconnoissance or demonstration, and it is very certain that could the original programme have been carried out the whole line would have been destroyed from Salkehatchie to Coosawhatchie. It proves the correctness of the information which I had previously gained, that the enemy was not in any considerable force at the railroad."

The expedition which General Stephens reported as "most successful," his commanding officer, General Benham, characterized as "a miserable failure."

The failure of this expedition to destroy the railroad did not retard or interfere with the main expedition to James Island. On the morning of June 2 General Stephens' command steamed out of Port Royal Harbor, and that evening entered the Stono and landed a little above Coles' Island, on Legare's plantation, on James Island, and brisk skirmishing immediately began. A detachment occupied Legareville on the left bank. Brigadier General H. G. Wright commanded a division on Edisto Island. At that point about seven thousand men of all arms had been concentrated. General Wright was ordered to pass this force over to Seabrook's Island and thence over Haulver Creek to John's Island, and from there to march directly to Legareville, on the Stono, and cross that river to take part with Stephens' Division in the coup-de-main. The mass of General Wright's command (it was designated as the First Division, but a part of General Stephens' Division—the Second—was with him) was on John's Island, near the Haulver, the night of the 2d. The distance from that point to Legareville, on the Stono, is about ten miles, and the road good. Captain Percival Drayton, of the navy, was in the Stono prepared to cross the troops over to James Island immediately on their arrival.

Some delay occurred in the movement of General Wright's command, attributed to the lack of transportation and a damaged wharf at Seabrook's Island. His command did not reach Legareville until the evening of the 5th. This delay, occurring after the arrival of Stephens' troops had given warning of the approaching storm, had given General Pemberton time, which it was believed he had profited by, to throw reinforcements on James Island. The purpose, therefore, of taking the island by a coup-de-main was abandoned and it was determined to hold the position already secured, provide a securely entrenched camp and await reinforcements. General Wright's division crossed the Stono on the 9th and took position on Mr. Thomas Grimble's plantation, two miles above General Stephens' command. The Confederates immediately opened fire of solid shot and shell, which fell into, around, and over General Wright's camp and among the gunboats in the Stono. General Stephens' camp was also under fire. This at once convinced General Benham that the main camps and landings were untenable while exposed to the Confederate fire, and as there was not dry land enough on the island above high water for a secure camp out of range of the Confederate guns, it seemed evident that he would be obliged to abandon the island,—the key to Charleston,—or silence the advanced Confederate batteries. On the 10th General Hunter, having determined to return to Hilton Head, gave to General Benham written instructions, in which he says:

"In leaving the Stono to return to Hilton Head,

I desire in any arrangement that you may make for the disposition of your forces now in this vicinity, you will make no attempt to advance on Charleston or attack Fort Johnson until largely reinforced, or until you receive specific instructions from these head-quarters to that effect. You will, however, provide for a secure, entrenched encampment, where your front can be covered by the fire of our gunboats from the Stono on the left and the creek from Folly River on the right."

The fire from the Confederate batteries continued to be very annoying on the 10th, so much so as to induce General Benham to make a move to put an end to it. He ordered a reconnoissance in force to be made on the Confederate works at the earliest dawn of day on the morning of the 11th. Picked regiments of General Stephens' division were to lead and "make a rush on the Confederate position," the remainder of Stephens' division being held close in hand to support the advance or follow up closely any advantage that might be gained. General Wright and Colonel Williams were to support Stephens on the left. The whole remaining force was to be held in readiness to give such strong and prompt support as to change the reconnoissance in force into a general engagement, if fortune favored and it should be found expedient. In that case Colonel Robert Williams was to lead the assaulting columns. Written instructions were prepared for Generals Wright and Stephens and Colonel Williams.

It seems that Generals Hunter and Benham had their headquarters temporarily on the same steamer,

the *Delaware,* in the Stono. Before issuing his instructions for the dash of the next day General Benham showed them to General Hunter, impressing
upon him at the same time the imperative necessity
of capturing or silencing the batteries at Secessionville. He also pointed out to General Hunter a line
traced on a map from Secessionville obliquely toward Charleston as the line which the Federal
troops should occupy to render their hold on James
Island secure, to all of which Benham says General
Hunter cordially assented, and on Benham's solicita-
tion Hunter agreed to defer his departure for Hilton
Head to await the result of the demonstration on
Secessionville. The line traced out as being the
proper one for the Union forces to occupy was already occupied by the Confederates, and it was
plainly necessary that the Federal troops must first
capture Secessionville and drive off the Confederates
before occupying it themselves. This contemplated
movement for the morning of the 11th was, however, deferred, because General Wright represented
that his troops were not in condition for action. General Hunter left the field of operations on the evening of the 11th, leaving General Benham in command, with the instructions already quoted.

Skirmishing had been brisk from the time of the
landing of the advance troops of the expedition.
From five to eight gunboats in the Stono and in a
creek flowing into Folly River had kept up a well-
sustained fire on the Confederate position. The
Federal commander had caused a battery of siege
guns to be constructed in front of General Stephens'

camp, to play upon the Confederate batteries in front of Secessionville. The skirmishing and the combined fire of the land and naval batteries were particularly spirited on Sunday, the 15th, but no perceptible effect was produced on the Confederate batteries. The enemy were known to be busily at work night and day, strengthening their positions, and it had been reported to General Benham some days before that from the masthead of a naval vessel in the Stono several long trains of cars loaded with troops had been seen pouring into Charleston over the road which Colonel Christ's expedition had failed to break. It therefore seemed manifest to General Benham that whatever he proposed to do to "provide a securely entrenched encampment" on James Island, as ordered by General Hunter, he should do quickly, without longer delay. He therefore determined to assault the Confederate position at the earliest dawn of day the next morning.

The plan of attack was substantially the same as that proposed to be made on the 10th, but on a larger scale. Generals Wright and Stephens, commanding divisions, and Colonel Robert Williams, commanding a brigade, were called in to confer with General Benham, and Captain Percival Drayton, of the navy, was invited to be present at the conference. The reports of what occurred in that conference are so conflicting that it is impossible to reconcile them.

This much seems certain, that General Stephens, whose division was designated to make the assault, strongly objected to the time of making it. He preferred to make it in the light of day, that his men

might see where they were required to go and what
was before them to be done. He advised that fire
be continued on the Confederate works, keeping the enemy constantly disturbed and uncertain as
to when and where the attack would be made, thus
wearying them out with watching, while the Federal
troops, their officers knowing exactly when the attack
would be made, could take their usual rest and regular meals and, when needed for action, would go
fresh to their work. Whatever objections were
raised were overruled by General Benham, who
ordered the assault to be made.

The consolidated morning reports of June 9
showed the Federal force in hand on James Island
to be: Wright's Division, 3232; Stephens' Division,
4313; Williams' Headquarters Brigade, 1927—
total, 9472. It was believed that the Confederate
force defending the works to be attacked was less
than 500 men. It was proposed to surprise that
force and capture the works.

General Stephens was ordered to form his entire
division before day dawn, secretly and in silence, at
the advanced picket line, and at day dawn, or about
four o'clock, to move rapidly upon the enemy's
works at and about Secessionville and carry them by
a coup-de-main. General Wright's Division, with
Williams' Brigade temporarily attached, was ordered to move at the same time from their camp at
Thomas Grimble's, to support Stephens and protect
his left and rear from any attack that might be made
by the Confederates from that direction. This precaution to guard against a flank and rear attack was

deemed so important that General Wright was ordered, in the event of Stephens being repulsed, not to renew the assault.

The Confederate works in front of Secessionville occupied the most contracted part of a narrow neck of land, with marshes fringed with brushwood on both sides. The route from General Stephens' camp to this position, after passing a causeway, was over cultivated fields, bordered with thorny hedges, the most advanced hedge being about five hundred yards from the Confederate batteries. The field in front of this hedge converged rapidly to the Confederate works, where the front of attack was about one hundred yards in length, flanked on either side by the before-mentioned marshes.

Stephens' Division was composed of two brigades of infantry, of three regiments each. The First Brigade, Colonel Fenton, Eighth Michigan, commanding, made up of the Eighth Michigan, Lieutenant Colonel F. Graves; the Seventh Connecticut, Lieutenant Colonel J. R. Hawley, and the Twenty-eighth Massachusetts, Lieutenant Colonel More, led the assault and was closely followed by the Second Brigade, Colonel Leasure, of the One Hundredth Pennsylvania, consisting of the Seventy-ninth New York Highlanders, Lieutenant Colonel David Morrison; the One Hundredth Pennsylvania, Lieutenant Colonel D. A. Lecky, and the Forty-sixth New York, Colonel Rudolph Rosa, commanding. A storming party, consisting of Companies C and H of the Eighth Michigan, Captains Ralph Ely and R. N. Doyle, led the assault, conducted by Lieutenant Lyons, aide-de-camp on General Stephens' staff, and followed by Captain Sears' company of New York Engineers. Rockwell's Battery of Connecticut Light Artillery followed the First Brigade and Captain Sargent's company of the First Massachusetts cavalry followed in the rear.

About four o'clock on a dark cloudy morning Stephens' whole command was in motion and, pressing forward rapidly and in silence, surprised the Confederate picket in the house they occupied, captured two or three of the men and, debouching through the advanced hedge, advancing at double-quick time, deployed, or attempted to deploy, intó line of battle, the Seventh Connecticut, the center regiment, following close on the Eighth Michigan, to form on its left. It seems that the mistake, or blunder, had been made of attempting to charge with brigade front over a space scarcely wide enough for a regiment in line. While the regiments of the leading brigade were forming forward into line in double-quick time a storm of grape and canister from the Confederate guns crashed through the center of the line and continued tearing through the ranks with great rapidity, severing the line, one part crowding toward the right, the other to the left. Says Lieutenant Colonel Graves:

"Still the regiment moved rapidly on, preserving their order and leaving the ground in their rear strewn with their dead and wounded, and did not stop until they gained the parapet and delivered their fire upon the enemy in his works. But they were unable to contend against such great odds, and, being entirely unsupported for a considerable time, they fell back slowly, contesting every inch of ground a short distance, where they maintained ground until ordered to retreat, which they did in good order, although under fire. The regiment, however, had become much scattered, owing to the great number of officers who had fallen."

The inevitable result of attempting to advance with brigade front over space hardly wide enough for a single regiment in line followed. The regiments became somewhat entangled with each other and the brushwood-fringed marshes on the flanks. When within two or three hundred yards of the Confederate works the Seventh Connecticut "came obliquely upon an unforeseen ditch and morass," crowding and doubling up the regiment toward the center. At this moment a terrific fire of grape and musketry swept through the ranks. "The line was inevitably broken," says Colonel Hawley, "and though the men stood bravely to their work the line could not be re-formed until the colors were brought into the open field. When re-formed it started again under a heavy fire toward the earthworks, but had proceeded but a little distance when an order came from General Stephens, brought by his son, who was then 'receiving his baptism of fire,' to call the men off, and the regiment fell back to the cover of the hedge in front of their hospital. The Twenty-eighth Massachusetts had been unavoidably pushed far to the left, and as soon as it was formed into line, advancing, one regiment that was in front fell back and broke through our regiment, throwing it into confusion.

"Forward again," he continues, "marched by the flank through a dense brush on our left and followed the edge of the bushes, which formed one side of a marsh to within forty yards of the enemy's work. Here our progress was interrupted by a large fallen tree, between which and the enemy's work was an impassable marsh. On our right was an abattis of dense brush and on our left and front marsh. Here we lost many of the men who were killed and wounded in the regiment. Seeing that we could be of no possible use in this place with less than platoon front to retaliate by fire on the enemy, and this position being raked by the fire of the gun on the corner of the enemy's work nearest the observatory, I ordered the regiment to retire,[2] and it, too, found shelter behind the hedge."

While the First Brigade was being thus cut up the Seventy-ninth Highlanders, leading the Second Brigade, was ordered by General Stephens to the right to assail the work a little to the right of the point from which the Eighth Michigan had been driven. Lieutenant Colonel Morrison led the right wing of his regiment to the parapet.

"As I mounted the parapet," says the Lieutenant Colonel, "I received a wound in the head, which, though slight, stunned me for the time being; but still I was able to retain command. With me many mounted the works, but only to fall or to receive

[2]Lieutenant Colonel Moore's report.

their wounds from the enemy, posted in rifle-pits in rear of the fort. . . . From the ramparts I had a full view of their works. They were entrenched in a position well selected for defensive purposes and upon which our artillery seemed to have little effect, save driving them into their retreats, and in attempting to dislodge them we were met with a fierce and determined opposition, but with equal if not superior determination and courage were they met by our forces, and had I been supported could have carried their works, . . . for we virtually had it in our possession. After remaining in this position some considerable time and not being supported by the other regiments, I received orders to fall back, which I did in good order, leaving behind about forty killed or badly wounded, many of whom fell on the ramparts, and brought back with me six killed and about sixty wounded," while the right companies of the regiment—"the left having encountered a perfect storm of grape and canister—were obliged to seek shelter either by obliquing to the left, under cover of a small ravine, or by dropping among the cotton ridges in front of the fort, where they kept up a steady fire on the enemy's gunners."[3]

Of the other two regiments of this brigade the One Hundredth Pennsylvania was formed in line of battle supporting the left of the Seventy-ninth Highlanders, and the Forty-sixth New York the left of the One Hundredth Pennsylvania. The brigade was thus formed in three lines of battle in echelon.

[3]Report of Colonel Leasure, commanding the brigade.

While the two latter regiments were coming into line, Colonel Leasure, the Brigade Commander, with his staff, hastened forward to hurry up the left of the Seventy-ninth, intending to lead the assault in person. When about three hundred yards from the Confederate works he reached the storm. He says:

"We entered the range of a perfect storm of grape, canister, nails, broken glass, and pieces of chains, fired from three very large pieces on the fort, which completely swept every foot of ground within the range, and either cut the men down or drove them to the shelter of the ravine on the left. I now turned to look after and lead up the One Hundredth Pennsylvania Regiment and found its center just entering the fatal line of fire, which completely cut it in two, and the right under Major Lecky obliqued to the right and advanced to support the right of the Seventy-ninth New York, and many of the men reached the foot of the embankment and some succeeded in mounting it, with a few brave men of the Seventy-ninth, who were there with a portion of the Eighth Michigan. . . .

"I may be permitted to report further that at the time I arrived in front of the hedge near the fort I saw nothing of any part of the supporting regiments of the First Brigade, and between the advancing Highlanders and the fort only a portion of the Eighth Michigan, who led the attack in front of the fort, that regiment having already been decimated by the murderous fire through which we all had to pass."

While the Forty-sixth New York was advancing

to the attack it was run into by parts of the Seventh
Connecticut and Twenty-eighth Massachusetts,
which were retreating, and swept along with them
in their retreat a part of the Forty-sixth New York.

"During all of this time our own artillery fired
over our heads from enormous distances and burst
several shells right over our heads. The fire of our
gunboats was also very disagreeable until they finally succeeded in getting a better range."

The First Brigade having utterly failed and fallen
back terribly shattered, the Second Brigade was re-
called and the whole division formed in two lines
near the points from which it had started. "My
men," says General Stephens, "were at the enemy's
works about 4:30 o'clock and the conflict of twenty-
five minutes, so dreadful in its casualties, was over
and the men returned." Rockwell's battery, or a
part of it, was pushed forward to the advanced
hedge and kept up a brisk fire on the fort, but the
assault had been made and failed disastrously.

General Wright's Division had moved promptly
at the appointed time and had well performed the
part assigned it. General Benham had joined
Wright about the time his division moved forward
and commanded in person. Receiving an urgent
request from General Stephens for support, Colonel
Williams was ordered to hasten forward with his
brigade and report to Stephens. His brigade approached the Confederate works to the left of the
marsh which had so cramped General Stephens' Division. It did not reach the point on which it was
directed until Stephens' attack had failed and his

division driven, or had fallen back, under cover. The Ninety-seventh Pennsylvania joined the left of Stephens' Division on the line to which it had fallen back. The Third New Hampshire and Third Rhode Island were pushed well to the front. The Third New Hampshire approached to within forty yards of the Confederate works and opened fire. Colonel Jackson, commanding the regiment, reports that he found no artillery on that part of the Confederate works and that he could easily have gone into the fort.

"If," he adds, "I could have crossed a stream between me and the earthworks about twenty yards in width, with apparently four or five feet of water, and the mud very soft; the men therefore could not cross. The enemy soon opened on me from a battery about two hundred yards in our rear, throwing grape into the ranks, from which we suffered severely. In a short time they opened fire with rifles and infantry. At the same time a battery about a mile north of us opened on us with shot and shell.

He seems to have been well enveloped in fire and the regiment suffered severely. He saw reinforcements passing into the Confederate works, which he was powerless to prevent. A section of Hamilton's battery—regular artillery—succeeded in silencing the battery in the rear and a battalion of the Third Rhode Island penetrated the brushwood to dislodge the Confederate sharpshooters, but did not succeed. The assault was already essentially over and it was a mere waste of life and limb to keep these troops where they were. They were therefore withdrawn.

General Stephens was holding his division, awaiting orders and ready to renew the assault, but no orders came and soon the whole Federal force on the island had returned to the camps from which they started. The aggregate Federal loss was 683. The Eighth Michigan had lost most heavily. It lost more than a third of the number engaged. Of twenty-two commissioned officers who went into action thirteen were killed or wounded. The Seventy-ninth Highlanders, Third New Hampshire, and Seventh Connecticut had also suffered severely. All the regiments actively engaged had lost seriously. Among the killed were: Captain Edwin S. Hitchcock and Lieutenant Thomas Hooton, Seventh Connecticut; Captains Benjamin B. Church and Simon Guild, Eighth Michigan; Captain Ralph Carlton, Third New Hampshire; Lieutenant Ferdinand Sehert, Forty-sixth New York; Lieutenant James Kinner, Seventy-ninth New York Highlanders, died on the 18th of wounds received; Lieutenant Samuel J. Moore, One Hundredth Pennsylvania, and Lieutenant Erasmus S. Bartholomew, Third Rhode Island Heavy Artillery.

The assault which had resulted so disastrously narrowly missed brilliant success. The works about Secessionville were occupied by two companies of the First (afterwards Second) South Carolina Artillery, and two battalions of infantry, the Charleston Battalion, Lieutenant Colonel Gaillard, and the Pee Dee Battalion, Lieutenant Colonel Smith commanding, in all less than five hundred men. Colonel T. G. Lamar, of the South Carolina Artillery, commanded the post. From the landing of the Federal force on the 2d to the morning of the 16th the Confederate troops had been subjected, day and night, to the most arduous duties. On the 15th there had been sharp skirmishing and the combined fire from the land and naval batteries had been unusually heavy. Notwithstanding the secrecy observed in the Federal camps, Colonel Lamar had observed enough to convince him that an attack would be made in the night of the 15th or early the following morning, and so reported to General Evans, commanding on the island, who ordered Colonel Johnson Hagood to reinforce Secessionville up to 2000 men, but the reinforcements had not arrived when the assault was made. Colonel Hagood carried the reinforcements without orders from General Evans. Colonel Lamar and his men had been busily at work all night of the 15th and until three o'clock in the morning constructing a new land battery and transferring guns to it from an old gunboat. About three o'clock in the morning the men, exhausted by the skirmishing of the day before and the labor of the night, were allowed to lie down to rest.

It was the first time since Colonel Lamar had been in command that his men had been allowed to sleep without arms in their hands and at the point where they would have to use them in the event of an attack. The men had scarcely fallen asleep when the storm of battle burst on them. Sending a courier to Colonels Gaillard and Smith, to hurry forward with their battalions, Colonel Lamar hastened to the

batteries, where the gunners were found at their
guns and alert. He was just in time to see in the
gray light of a cloudy morning the enemy's line advancing at the double-quick to the assault.

Mounting the chasee of the ten-inch columbiad,
he aimed it himself at the center of the advancing
line, to break and delay it until the infantry support
could come up. Immediately all of the guns were
firing, the columbiad and eighteen-pounders firing
grape and canister, the twenty-four-pounders firing
solid shot and shells. The fire on the center of the
line had, as we have seen, the desired effect of breaking it and causing a little delay, and when the leading regiment, the Eighth Michigan, reached the
ditch and mounted to the parapet it encountered a
storm of fire from Colonel Smith's Pee Dee Battalion, and after a brief and fierce struggle the
Eighth Michigan, as has been seen, was driven back,
badly shattered. The Charleston Battalion, under
Lieutenant Colonel Gaillard, followed closely on the
heels of the Pee Dee Battalion and was put into
action on the right of the battery. When the Michigan regiment fell back Colonel Smith sallied out and
gathered up the arms (they were better than his
own) which had fallen from the hands of the killed
and wounded, and put them in the hands of his own
men in time to use them in repelling the assault of
the Seventy-ninth Highlanders. Early in the assault
a detachment of one hundred men of the Twenty-
second South Carolina, sent to reinforce the garrison, arrived and took an active part in the defense.
A little later Lieutenant Colonel McEnery arrived

with his Louisiana Battalion and also took an active part in repelling the last assault.

That night Colonel Stevens, of the Twenty-fourth South Carolina Regiment, commanded the picket line of Hagood's Brigade. It consisted of seven companies of the Twenty-fourth and six of the First South Carolina Regiment and one of the Forty-seventh Georgia Regiment. The picket line, connecting on the left with the picket in front of Secessionville, covered the whole Confederate front to Newtown Cut. As soon as the Federal advance was made known to Colonel Hagood he sent McEnery's Louisiana Battalion to Secessionville and carried the remainder of his brigade not already on outpost duty to the picket line, to the felled timber near the Battery Island road. One of Captain Boyce's six-pounder guns was placed in battery on the left of the felled timber, which made good abattis. About one hundred of Colonel Stevens' pickets already occupied a thicket extending from the felled timber to the morass on the left near the Secessionville batteries. The Twenty-fifth South Carolina, Colonel Simonton, was in rear of the felled timber and to the right of the field piece.

Lieutenant Colonel Capers commanded the battery at Clark's House, which, though at a greater distance than the other batteries, was most effectively served. These were the troops (Hagood's Brigade) that almost enveloped the Third New Hampshire and repulsed a very gallant and determined dash made by a battalion of the Third Rhode Island Heavy Artillery to dislodge the troops in the felled timber and capture the gun which was galling the rear of the Third New Hampshire. Colonel Williams' Brigade was plainly seen by Colonel Hagood in line of battle about Hill's Houses. He immediately dispatched an officer to General Evans, commanding on the island, asking to be supported in making an attack on the flank and rear of Williams' Brigade. But before permission to attack and assurance of support were received Colonel Williams' Brigade was withdrawn, the whole Federal force on the island returned to the camp from which it had started before the first dawn of day, and the assault of Secessionville was ended.

The aggregate Confederate loss was 204, nearly the whole of it falling on the troops who defended the Secessionville batteries. The struggle for the parapet had been especially stubborn and fierce. Muskets were clubbed and Lieutenant Campbell and Mr. Tennant, of the Charleston Battalion, in default of better weapons, seized handspikes and wielded them with effect. Among the killed were Captain Samuel J. Reed, First South Carolina Artillery; Captain Henry C. King and Lieutenant John J. Edwards, of the Charleston Battalion; Lieutenant B. A. Graham, of the Forty-seventh Georgia, and Richard W. Greer, of the Twenty-fifth South Carolina.

As soon as the result of the assault was made known to General Hunter, then at Hilton Head, he relieved General Benham from command and ordered him to Washington in arrest, charged with disobedience of orders and instructions in making the assault. General Wright, who succeeded General Benham in command, was ordered to abandon James Island, which was soon done, leisurely and in perfect order. The Federal troops returned to the points from which they had started on the expedition and the Confederates were left undisturbed to complete the strong lines of earthworks on James Island from Fort Johnson, on the harbor, to Pringle, on the Stono, which were never captured.

CHAPTER VII

Operations on the South Atlantic Coast—General Hunter's policy
—Expedition up the St. John's—Capture of St. John's
Bluff—General Hunter is succeeded by Major General
Ormesby Mitchell—Expedition toward Pocotaligo—Engage-
ment at Frampton's plantation and Pocotaligo—Negro
troops—General Saxton's activities—Contraband.

While the Union troops under the command of
Brigadier General H. G. Wright were withdrawing
from James Island after the failure of the assault
of June 16 on Secessionville, there was urgent need
for reinforcements in both the Union and Confederate armies in other quarters.

In Virginia the battles of Fair Oaks and Seven
Pines had been followed by the seven days' battles
around Richmond; General McClellan's army had
been pressed back to Harrison's Landing on the
James, and General Lee was preparing to throw his
army against the Army of Northern Virginia, and
by threatening Washington recall General McClellan from the prosecution of operations against the
Confederates, to the defense of the Union capital.
West of the Mississippi the battle of Pea Ridge had
been fought, and to the east of it the sanguinary and
indecisive battle of Shiloh had been followed by the
slow but steady advance of the army under General
Halleck toward Corinth, until General Beauregard

117

was forced to face back to Tupelo. General Buell, commanding the Army of the Ohio, detached from General Halleck's army, was marching eastward to seize the important strategic point of Chattanooga, while General Bragg, who had succeeded General Beauregard in command, was preparing to transfer his army to the same point, anticipate General Buell in its occupation, and to march thence into Kentucky. These military operations had been attended with fearfully heavy losses in the various armies engaged.

In response to a call from the War Department for reinforcements, General Hunter sent seven regiments of infantry and a few companies of the First Massachusetts Cavalry to Virginia, under Brigadier General I. I. Stearns. So large a draft on his force reduced it to that degree that General Hunter was not only unable to renew offensive operations against Charleston, but could not make any formidable demonstration at any point on the mainland. Operations along the coast were therefore reduced to predatory excursions by small parties and surprises and skirmishes between the advanced pickets.

General Hunter availed himself of this enforced lull in active military operations in his own department to inaugurate a favorite plan of his, from which he anticipated the happiest results. His predecessor, General W. T. Sherman, had been embarrassed, rather than aided, by the number of negroes who had been brought under his care and control by the occupation of some, and the exposed condition of all of the sea islands and the adjacent mainland.

General Hunter had, on May 9, without authority from his Government, issued a General Order emancipating all of the slaves in the States of South Carolina, Georgia, and Florida, and proceeded to arm, equip, and organize into companies and regiments the able-bodied negro men under his control, to be used in the prosecution of the war in those States. His method of recruiting was most arbitrary and summary. He ordered all able-bodied negro men capable of bearing arms, and within the limits of his command, to be sent under guard to his headquarters. The soldiers were employed to enforce the order, and marched to different plantations, took charge of the negroes, at work in the fields or whenever they could be found, and hurried them off to headquarters, without giving them time to go to their cabins for necessary clothing or to make any preparation for their sudden transition from the cotton field to the ranks of the army. The order produced the wildest consternation and panic among the negroes. Many of them fled from their homes and concealed themselves in the woods, where they were pursued by the soldiers, and those of them who could be found were forcibly brought in and hurried off to Hilton Head, "sighing for the old fetters as being better than the new liberty," says Mr. Wells, one of the Northern overseers in charge of a plantation.

The time, however, had not yet arrived for resorting to that measure for crippling the South and swelling the ranks of the Union armies. President Lincoln repudiated and revoked General Hunter's orders, not, however, until the latter had organized one regiment of negroes,—the first of some forty-eight thousand or fifty thousand of such troops that he expected to organize during the summer and autumn.

It was plainly desirable that the negroes left by their owners on the abandoned plantations should be organized and brought under some control, and direction made for the cultivation of those productive islands. Brigadier General Rufus Saxton, an ardent advocate of the plan for giving arms and military organization to the slaves, and using them in the prosecution of the war in that quarter, had been assigned to the special duty of organizing and directing the negroes in the cultivation of the abandoned plantations. He was clothed with full authority over all the inhabitants—who were not in the military service of the United States—of that part of the country within the Union lines, or that might be brought within them in the prosecution of the war. In ordering courts-martial for the trial of all offenders, and taking final action on the cases tried, his authority was the same as that vested in generals commanding armies or military departments. He was further authorized to organize and arm five thousand negro men, and muster them in for the war for service in the Quartermaster General's Department, and five thousand to be organized into companies, regiments, and brigades. They were to be officered by white men selected from the regiments then in service, and were to be armed and uniformed and received into the service with the same pay and allowances as other troops of the line. They were to be employed in guarding and protecting negroes who were engaged in the cultivation of the plantations, to make forays into the country and bring away all negroes of what condition soever, and to destroy all property which might be useful in the prosecution of the war that could not be brought within the Union lines. Thus provision was made for raising a quasi-army of ten thousand men, in addition to the force already in the department, and to be under the command of Brigadier General Saxton.

On September 5 General Hunter left the department on a long leave of absence, and was succeeded in command on September 17 by Major General Ormesby M. Mitchell, Brigadier General J. M. Brannan commanding in the interim.

During the brief period of his command General Mitchell infused some new life and activity into the military operations of his department.

In the preceding May General H. G. Wright, whose brigade had occupied St. Augustine and parts of Florida bordering on the St. John's River, was withdrawn, with his command, to take part in the general movements for the capture of Charleston. On the withdrawal of the troops the Floridians returned to their homes in Jacksonville and other points. Some Confederate troops also occupied that part of the country and were engaged in placing it in condition of defense. A battery of some strength had been constructed in and armed at St. John's Bluff, on the river of that name.

On September 30 General Mitchell dispatched General Brannan to the St. John's River with the Forty-seventh Pennsylvania and Seventh Connecticut Infantry, a section of the First Connecticut Artillery, and a detachment of the First Massachusetts Cavalry, in all 1568 men. On the way he was joined by a fleet of six gunboats, Captain Charles Steedman commanding. The expedition entered the St. John's in the afternoon of the next day. Three gunboats proceeded to reconnoiter the battery on the bluff, and after a brisk engagement retired out of range. Under cover of the naval vessels the troops landed at Mayport Mills, but ascertaining there that, owing to intervening creeks and marshes, it would be necessary to march about forty miles to reach the rear of St. John's Bluff, General Brannan moved his command in boats, furnished from the fleet, higher up and landed the infantry at Burkbone Creek, between Publo and Mount Pleasant. Early on the morning of the 2d Colonel Good of the Forty-seventh Pennsylvania moved with the infantry of the command and the naval howitzers to the head of Mount Pleasant Creek, drove from their camp a Confederate picket, and occupied a position about two miles from St. John's Bluff, to cover the landing of the detachments of artillery and cavalry. Receiving information which he regarded as reliable, that there were 1200 Confederate infantry and cavalry between him and the Bluff, General Brannan, after consultation with Captain Steedman, called upon Colonel Rice, commanding the Ninth Maine at Fernandina, for reinforcement, and 300 men were promptly dispatched to him. Late in the afternoon of the 3d Captain Steedman, at General Brannan's request, sent three gunboats to feel the battery at the Bluff. Finding, to his surprise, that it was not occupied, he sent a boat party ashore, which hoisted the Union flag over the Confederate battery.

While General Brannan was waiting within two miles of the Bluff for the arrival of reinforcements, the battery had been for eighteen or twenty hours wide open to receive him. As so often happened during the war, each commander had greatly over-estimated his adversary's force.

Lieutenant Colonel Charles F. Hopkins had been assigned to the command of the Bluff a few days (September 26) before the appearances of the Union force in the river. In addition to the gunners who manned the battery, he had outside for its defense on the land front a mixed force of about 500, instead of 1200. Colonel Hopkins, who from his position in the battery had watched the landing of a part of the force, judging from what he had himself seen and from information brought him by the picket that had been driven in, estimated the Union land force at 3000 men, whereas it was but little more than half that number. Feeling his inability to defend his post against a combined attack of the troops which he estimated outnumbered him by six to one, and the six gunboats in the river in his front, Colonel Hopkins, with the concurrence of the officers of his command whom he consulted, abandoned the battery about nine o'clock on the night of the 2d; and not having the means of removing his heavy guns and ammunition, and fearing that any attempt to burst or otherwise disable them would apprise the enemy of his intended retreat, left them all uninjured. While General Brannan was surprised at his good fortune in gaining possession, without striking a blow, of a post strong by nature and strengthened by well-planned and constructed works, Colonel Hopkins congratulated himself on having saved his small force from capture.[1]

After moving the guns and ammunition to a transport, blowing up the magazine, and destroying the entire work, General Brannan proceeded up the river to Jacksonville, which he found deserted, the inhabitants, with the exception of a few old men, women, and children, having abandoned their homes on the approach of the enemy and moved back in the interior. While at Jacksonville a small party was sent in a transport, escorted by a gunboat, about 230 miles up the river, and took possession of a small abandoned steamer, the *Governor Milton*. On October 13 the whole expedition had returned to Hilton Head. The return had been hastened by General Mitchell, who proposed himself to lead a more extensive expedition against the Charleston & Savannah Railroad.

The force designated for this expedition was parts of the First Brigade, Brigadier General J. M. Brannan's, and of the Second Brigade, Brigadier General A. H. Terrie's, augmented by detachments of other organizations, making a total land force of 4450

---

[1] A court of inquiry which he demanded exonerated him from all blame.

men.[2] Several boat howitzers manned by officers and men of the navy were added to the land force.

The gunboats and transports of the expedition were under command of Captain Charles Steedman, United States Navy.

The organization of the command and all of the details as to transportation, supplies, and ammunition had been made entirely by Major General Mitchell, who had intended to command it in person. A few hours before it sailed, however, Brigadier General Brannan was assigned to the command, Colonel Chatfield of the Sixth Connecticut succeeding to the command of his brigade. The object of the expedition was to destroy the railroad and bridges on the Charleston & Savannah Road, and the points of attack were Coosawhatchie and Poco-

[2] The troops composing the expedition were the following: Forty-seventh Pennsylvania Volunteers, 600 men, Colonel Tolghman H. Good; Fifty-fifth Pennsylvania Volunteers, 400 men, Colonel Richard White; Fourth New Hampshire Volunteers, 500 men (Colonel Chatfield) Lieutenant Colonel Spidel; Seventh Connecticut Volunteers, 500 men, Colonel Joseph R. Hawley; Third New Hampshire Volunteers, 480 men, Colonel John H. Jackson; Seventy-sixth Pennsylvania Volunteers, 430 men, Colonel DeWitt C. Strawbridge; Forty-eighth New York Volunteers, 200 men, Colonel William B. Barton; First New York Mechanics and Engineers, 250 men, Lieutenant Colonel James F. Hall; a section of Battery M, First United States Artillery, 40 men, Lieutenant Guy V. Henry; a section of Hamilton's Battery E, Second United States Artillery, Lieutenant E. Gittings; detachment of the First Massachussetts Cavalry, 100 men, Captain L. Richmond. A total force of 4500. Colonel Edward W. Serrgie, First New York Engineers, served on General Brannan's staff.

taligo, two stations on the road about ten miles apart. Scouts and spies had been sent by General Mitchell to the most important points on the line of the railroad, from the Savannah to the Salke-hatchie rivers, a distance of sixty miles. Small parties were also sent in boats up the Coosawhatchie, Tulli-finnie, and Pocotaligo, to ascertain and report the depth of water and condition of the different land-ings. A party was sent in advance to cut the tele-graph wires, and every precaution taken to insure success. Mackey's Point, a narrow neck of land be-tween the Pocotaligo and Broad rivers, was selected as the place for landing—a judicious selection, as gunboats in the two streams could thoroughly sweep the ground some miles in front and securely cover the landing.

The expedition started from Hilton Head in the night of the 21st, in fourteen gunboats and armed transports, and the leading vessel reached Mackey's Point about half-past four o'clock the next morning. It was eight o'clock before the other vessels arrived. Colonel Barton, with fifty men of the New York Engineers and fifty of the Third Rhode Island Vol-unteers was immediately sent up the Coosawhatchie in the steamer *Planter*, which had been converted into a heavily armed gunboat, accompanied by two other gunboats, to destroy the railroad and bridges at and near the village of Coosawhatchie. The main body, under cover of the batteries of the gunboats, landed without opposition at Mackey's Point, seven or eight miles from Old Pocotaligo, and marched forward over a good road up the narrow neck of land between the Tullifinnie and Pocotaligo, which securely protected the flanks, while the gunboats covered the rear of the column.

Brigadier General W. S. Walker, C. S. A.,[3] commanded in the military district invaded, with headquarters at McPhersonville, via the railroad about ten miles from Coosawhatchie toward Charleston. It was not until 9 A. M. that his pickets informed him of the landing of the expedition at Mackey's Point and the passage of gunboats up the Coosawhatchie. His small force was distributed over a distance of sixty miles along and near the railroad. The general plan for the protection of the road and that part of the country was to occupy the most vulnerable points by as large detachments as the small available force could supply; these detachments to be quickly concentrated at the menaced point, and hold the enemy in check until reinforcements could arrive from Charleston and Savannah, and any other point from which they could be spared. General Walker's measures for defense were taken with the promptness which characterized him. The troops nearest McPhersonville were ordered to Old Pocotaligo, about five miles from Coosawhatchie. The Lafayette Artillery, four pieces; Lieutenant L. F. LeBeau's, and a section of the Beaufort Artillery, Lieutenant H. M. Stuart commanding, were ordered to Coosawhatchie. Captain Wyman's company, Eleventh South Carolina, which was near the village, and five other companies of the same regiment at Hardieville were

[3] He was a colonel at the time, but was promoted a few days later.

ordered up to support the artillery. Colonel Colcock's command of five companies of cavalry and
two of sharpshooters, in front of Grahamville, was
ordered to Coosawhatchie. Major J. R. Jefford's
battalion of cavalry (Seventh South Carolina) was
ordered from Green Pond to the Salkehatchie Bridge,
and calls were made on Savannah, Charleston, and
Adams Run for reinforcements; those from Charleston and Adams Run to stop at Pocotaligo Station,
those from Savannah at Coosawhatchie. Captain
W. L. Trenholm, who commanded the outpost nearest Mackey's Point, was ordered to fall back with
his command of two mounted companies, his own
(the Rutledge Mounted Riflemen) and Captain M.
J. Kirk's company of Partisan Rangers toward Old
Pocotaligo.

When these dispositions were made General
Walker had with him to meet the advancing enemy
two sections of Beaufort Light Artillery and the Nel-
son (Virginia) Light Battery, eight pieces, Captain
Stephen Elliott commanding; Captain Trenholm's
two companies; the Charleston Light Dragoons,
Captain B. H. Rutledge; the First Battalion South
Carolina Cavalry, Major J. H. Morgan; Captain
D. B. Heywood's company of cavalry; Captain J. B.
Allston's company of sharpshooters, and Captain
A. C. Izard's company of the Eleventh South Carolina Infantry, numbering in all 475 men, and as a
fourth of the mounted men were horse-holders, his
effective force was but 405 men. Of this force a
section of the Beaufort Artillery, supported by two
companies of cavalry under Major Morgan and All-

ston's company of sharpshooters, was sent forward
to Caston's plantation to skirmish with and retard
the enemy, while the remaining troops took a strong
position on the Mackey's Point road at a salt marsh
skirted on both sides by woods traversed by a small
stream and crossed by a causeway near Dr. Hutson's
residence on the Frampton plantation.

Colonel Barton ascended the river in the *Planter,*
followed by the gunboats, to within about two miles
of Coosawhatchie, where he landed and marched
forward, driving the enemy's pickets before him.
When within a few hundred yards of the village a
train of cars was heard approaching, and he quickly
placed his little command in ambush. It was the
train which was bringing the troops ordered up from
Hardeeville for the defense of Coosawhatchie.
When it came within easy range Colonel Barton's
command poured into it a destructive fire of musketry and canister from the boat howitzers, inflicting
serious loss among the men crowded together on the
platform cars. Among the killed were the commander of the party, Major J. J. Harrison, and the
fireman of the train. The engineer was badly
wounded, but stood to his post and dashed his train
at full speed through the fire.

Leaving Captain Eaton of the New York Engineers with a party of his men to tear up the road
and cut down and destroy the telegraph line, Colonel
Barton hastened forward to the village to attack
the troops while in the confusion of leaving the train.
But when he came in sight of the village he saw the
artillery advantageously posted and supported by

a company of infantry on the further side of the stream, between the railroad and public bridges, their flanks protected on their left by the river and right by a swamp. The artillery immediately opened fire, to which Colonel Barton replied by a few rounds. But night was coming on, the reinforcements in the ambushed train had arrived, and finding himself in front of a much superior force Colonel Barton drew off his men and returned to his gunboats. Captain Eaton had succeeded in cutting the telegraph line in several places and tearing up two rails, and while toiling at others some cavalry videttes appeared at a little distance, and he too drew off, joining the rest of the command, and returned to the gunboats, destroying on the way four bridges to retard pursuit.

Colonel Colcock, who was so prostrated by a protracted fever that he could not take the field, ordered Lieutenant Colonel Johnson to take the command with the utmost dispatch to Coosawhatchie. On the way Lieutenant Colonel Johnson was deceived first by a report that reached him that the enemy had landed at Seabrook's Island, indicating that the attack was to be made at Grahamville; then by another that they were marching on Bees Creek Hill. His movements to meet the altered conditions of affairs as indicated by these erroneous reports so delayed him that, when he ascertained that the Union force was really marching on Coosawhatchie, he was obliged to make a detour of five miles to reach that place. When he arrived the little party under Colonel Barton had retreated and, the bridges having been torn up, Colonel Johnson did not come up with them until they were embarking, when a brisk fire was exchanged with some effect, Lieutenant J. B. Blanding, Third Rhode Island Artillery, who was in charge of the *Planter*, being among the severely wounded. But the batteries of the gunboat kept the Confederate cavalry at too great a distance for effective fire, and Colonel Barton dropped down the river to the point from which he had started.

While Colonel Barton was carrying out his part of the general plan, General Brannan's column moved forward on the Mackey's Point road, and after marching about 5½ miles and debouching upon an open, rolling country, it was fired upon by the section of the Beaufort Artillery and its support in position, as has been said, at Caston's plantation. The First Brigade, in advance, was promptly deployed, the artillery hastened to the front, and after a brisk artillery duel, in which Major Morgan, commanding the Confederate support, was severely wounded, the First Brigade advanced and the Confederate advance guard fell back to the position occupied by General Walker at the Frampton plantation, closely followed by the Union column. The Confederate position was naturally strong. The ground was firmer and somewhat more elevated than that on the other side that the Union column soon reached. Thick woods screened it and concealed the Confederate weakness in numbers. The swamp in front was broad and deep, traversed by a small stream, and passable only by a narrow causeway, as the bridge over the little stream had been broken.

On the Union side the marsh was fringed with timber and covered by a dense thicket. The eight Confederate field pieces were in batteries on an arc of a curve giving them a concentric fire on the causeway and the woods on either side of it.

When the head of the first brigade came within range a rapid artillery fire opened upon it; the two sections of United States artillery and the naval battery were hurried forward into position, and a rapid and well directed fire was maintained on both sides, until the Union ammunition was nearly exhausted. In the meantime the infantry of the first brigade struggled with steady courage and determination to penetrate the woods and thicket, cross the marsh, and reach the Confederate position on the further side, but in vain. Twice it was driven out of the woods with heavy loss. The Forty-seventh Pennsylvania and Sixth Connecticut, which were in advance, suffered most severely, the former losing nearly a fifth of its men. Colonel Chatfield, commanding the brigade, and Lieutenant Colonel Speidel, commanding the Sixth Connecticut, were among the severely wounded, the command of the brigade devolving on Colonel Good of the Forty-seventh Pennsylvania.

At the first sound of the artillery fire General Terry led his brigade at the double quick to the support of the first. The Seventy-sixth Pennsylvania of this brigade was thrown into the woods on the left of the road to support the left of the first brigade, which was still striving to force its way through the marsh. Knowing no way by which the Confed-

erate position could be turned, General Brannan
placed Lieutenant Henry's section of the First Artillery, well supported, in a position on the left of the
causeway, from which a more effective fire could be
delivered, and again pressed his infantry through
the woods, so far that the infantry fire was having
a most destructive effect on the men and horses of
the Confederate artillery. That arm seems to have
been General Walker's main reliance, and was already so badly cut up that he deemed it advisable to
withdraw to another strong position at the crossing
of the Pocotaligo, about 2½ miles in his rear. This
was done in good order, Captain Allston's company
of sharpshooters and Lieutenant Campell's, of the
Eleventh South Carolina, covering the retreat. The
infantry of Brannan's first brigade promptly plunged
through the marsh, "up to the men's arm-pits" in
mud and water, and pressed forward in pursuit. The
little bridge was quickly so repaired by the engineers
as to permit the passage of the artillery, when the
remaining force passed over and followed in pursuit.

It was all-important to General Walker to hold
his enemy in check until reinforcements which he
was expecting could arrive. The object of General
Brannan's expedition was to reach the railroad and
destroy as much of it as possible. When he reached
the juncture of the Mackey's Point with the Coosawhatchie road, it would seem that if, instead of
following and attacking General Walker in his new
position, he had marched directly forward a mile or
so over a comparatively open and practicable
country, he could have struck the bridge and trestle

work about the Tullifinnie, where his engineer troops
could have accomplished much destruction in a very
short time. He, however, left a regiment and howitzer to guard his flank and rear from that direction,
and followed the retreating Confederates to their
new position on the further side of the Pocotaligo,
where the men were sheltered by the houses and scattered trees of the little hamlet. The bridge over
the stream, which was approached by a causeway
over another marsh, was torn up and the artillery,
now much reduced, was in position to command the
causeway and crossing. Two pieces of the Beaufort artillery had been silenced by the killing and
wounding of the gunners, and but two of the guns
were serviceable. The Nelson Battery had suffered
even more severely in killed and wounded, the two
Lieutenants, E. E. Jefferson and F. T. Massey, being
among the wounded; it had but seventeen serviceable horses; one caisson had been broken by the
running away of the team early in the action at
Frampton's, and was left on the field. The ammunition happened to fit the naval howitzers, and was
returned to the Confederates at Pocotaligo from the
muzzles of those guns. Other pieces had been disabled, and only one could be brought into action in
the new position. General Walker had scarcely
made his dispositions for defense when the Union
column came in sight and the fighting was renewed
with spirit.

As at Frampton's, the Union troops endeavored,
but in vain, to cross the marsh. On a call for volunteers to find a way through, a party of men stepped

forward, and between the two fires scattered through the marsh seeking a practicable passage through it, but were unsuccessful. On another call a lieutenant and sergeant penetrated to the little river and, returning, reported that, like other streams of the country, though narrow, it was deep and the banks steep and muddy.

The Union batteries had exhausted their ammunition, and the caissons not having accompanied the guns, the latter were sent back to Mackey's Point, seven or eight miles, to replenish their ammunition chests. In the absence of the artillery the Sharps' breech-loading rifles were used with great rapidity and effect. General Walker had been notified by telegraph that reinforcements were on the way to him from Charleston, Savannah, and Adams Run. The Nelson Battalion (Seventh South Carolina) of 200 men, Captain W. H. Sleigh, commanding, arrived between four and five o'clock, but scarcely more than filled the gaps already made in the ranks. It was the only reinforcements that arrived in time to take part in the engagement. Its arrival encouraged and in a measure relieved the men who had been fighting and retreating for six hours. They were received with hearty cheers as they double-quicked into position. About the same time the Charleston Light Dragoons, which had been held in reserve, were ordered up, and came into position on the left with an inspiring shout. The cheering produced the impression that reinforcements in considerable number were arriving. A piece of the Beaufort artillery, with a small support, was moved by a concealed route to a position which suggested to General Brannan that it was a movement to turn his left flank. His ammunition was nearly exhausted, and there was none nearer than Mackey's Point, and night was coming on. Recognizing the hopelessness of attempting anything further against a force which he believed (erroneously) was much larger than his own, and in a strong position, General Brannan ordered a retreat to Mackey's Point, which was made deliberately and in good order. He was unprovided with "sufficient transportation to remove the wounded, who were lying writhing along our entire route," he says. Nevertheless the killed were generally buried and the wounded removed on improvised stretchers. The bridges which had been torn up by the retreating and repaired by the advancing troops earlier in the day were again destroyed to retard pursuit. But the Confederates were in no condition for vigorous pursuit. They had lost 163 of the 475 men present when the fighting began, and had received but 200 men as reinforcements. The Union loss was 340. The following day the troops of the expedition re-embarked at Mackey's Point and returned to their respective stations.

General Brannan was under the impression that in these engagements he had encountered superior numbers, and two weeks later on, November 6, in a General Order complimenting his troops for their gallantry and good conduct on the expedition to Pocotaligo, he tells them that "though laboring under many disadvantages, yet by superior courage and determination was a greater force of the rebels driven from their strong and well studied positions at Caston's and Frampton's, and pursued flying and in confusion to their intrenchments on the Pocotaligo"; whereas, as has been seen, from the firing of the first to the last shot of the day he had outnumbered his adversary from nine to ten to one.

This was the last expedition of any magnitude undertaken in the Department of the South until the next spring. On October 30 Major General Mitchell died of fever at Beaufort, and General Brannan succeeded by seniority to the command of the department. His aggregate force present when he assumed command was but 12,838.

General Saxton, who as superintendent of abandoned plantations and director of the negroes within the Union lines, exercised an independent command within a command, reporting directly to the Secretary of War, seems to have been thoroughly imbued with the belief that the heaviest blow against the South could be struck by negroes armed and organized into a military force. And there were officers about him who shared that belief. His plan was to haul a number of light-draught steamers well armed and protected against rifle shots. Each steamer was to have on hand a company of one hundred negro soldiers, whom he regarded as better fitted for the particular service required of them than white soldiers. An abundant supply of muskets and ammunition was to be placed in the hands of the negroes who might be gathered and found capable of bearing arms. These boats should be sent up the bays, lagoons, and streams intersecting the Southern coast, some of which were navigable for more than a hundred miles into the heart of the richest part of the Southern country. They should land at the various plantations, drive off the owners or any pickets that might be found, and bring away the negroes. Those who were capable of bearing arms were to be placed in the ranks. This species of warfare he thought would carry terror to the hearts of the Southerners. "In this way," he writes to the Secretary of War, "we could very soon have complete occupation of the whole country. Indeed, I can see no limit to which our success might not be pushed—up to the entire occupation of States, or their occupation by a large portion of the rebel army."

The organization of a negro regiment called the First South Carolina Union Infantry had been commenced, the officers being white men selected from the volunteer regiments. With these troops General Saxton undertook on a small scale to carry his plan into execution.

On November 3 he dispatched Lieutenant Colonel Oliver T. Beard, of the Forty-eighth New York Volunteers, in command of a detachment of the First South Carolina Regiment on an expedition along the coast of Georgia and east Florida, between Saint Simon's Island and Fernandina; and again on November 13 to the Doboy River, Georgia. On both expeditions he was accompanied by a naval gunboat. Lieutenant Colonel Beard's official reports are brief and to the point, and will illustrate the species of warfare carried on by General Saxton on the Southern coast in the autumn and winter of 1862-3.

Reporting to General Saxton, Colonel Beard says: " . . . On Monday, November 3, with the steamer *Darlington,* having on board Captain Trobridge's company of colored troops (Sixty-second), I proceeded up Bell River, Florida, drove in the rebel pickets below Cooper's and destroyed their place of rendezvous; thence proceeded and destroyed the salt works and all the salt, corn, and wagons which we could not carry away, besides killing the horses; thence we proceeded to Jolly River and destroyed two salt works, with a large amount of salt and corn; thence proceeded to Saint Mary's and brought off two families of contrabands, after driving in the enemy's pickets.

"On Tuesday, November 4, I proceeded to Kings Bay, Georgia, and destroyed a large salt work on a creek about a mile from the landing, together with all the property on the place. Here we were attacked by about eighty of the enemy, of whom we killed two.

"On Thursday, November 6, landed on Butler Island and brought off eighty bushels of rice; also landed at Darien and captured three prisoners and some arms.

"Friday, November 7, accompanied by the gunboat *Potemska,* Lieutenant Budd commanding, proceeded up Sapello River. The gunboat could proceed no further than Kings. Lieutenant Budd came on board the *Darlington* and proceeded up the river with us to Fairhope. At Spauldings we were attacked by eighty or ninety of the enemy, who were well posted on a bluff behind trees. At this point the channel runs within fifty yards of the bluff. We killed two of the enemy and had one colored man wounded. At Fairhope we destroyed the salt works, some ten vats, corn, and other things that might be of use to the enemy.

"On return past Spaulding's we were again attacked by the enemy in greater force. We effected a landing and burned all the buildings on the place and captured some arms, etc. Five of the enemy were killed; we lost three wounded. We were greatly aided here by the *Potemska*, which from a bend below shelled the woods. Under the guns of the *Potemska* we landed at Colonel Brailsford's, drove in a company of pickets from his regiment, and destroyed all the property on the place, together with the most important buildings.

.   .   .   .   .   .

I started from Saint Simons with sixty-two fighting men and returned to Beaufort with 156 fighting men (all colored) . . .

"We destroyed nine large salt works, together with twenty thousand dollars' worth of horses, salt, rice, corn, etc., which we could not carry away."

Again reporting the result of his expedition to Doboy River, Georgia, he says: "I succeeded in loading the steamers *Ben DeFord* and *Darlington* with from 200,000 to 300,000 feet of superior boards and planks, besides securing a number of circular and other saws, belting, corn mills, and other property which I was directed to obtain for your department."

In the following January Colonel T. W. Higginson (of Massachusetts), commanding the First South Carolina Colored Infantry, carried his regiment on a similar expedition up the Saint Mary's River in Georgia and Florida, in three steamers, the result of which he reported to General Saxton as successful beyond his most sanguine expectations. He discovered and brought away much valuable property, and left undisturbed much valuable household furniture, which he forbade his officers and men to take. "No wanton destruction was permitted, nor were any buildings burned, unless in retaliation for being fired upon, according to the usages of war.

.   .   .   .   .

Nothing was taken for public use save articles strictly contraband of war."

Among the articles which he seems to regard as belonging to that class, and which he brought away, were "40,000 large-sized bricks, four horses, four steers, and a quantity of agricultural implements suitable for Mr. Helper's operations at this locality." He also found great quantities "of choice Southern lumber," and brought away as much of it as he could; but he left behind more than 1,000,000 feet of choice lumber, "for want of transportation," the three steamboats under his control being laden to their full capacity with other freight. The conduct of his negro troops greatly surprised and filled him with the most enthusiastic admiration for their gallantry and peculiar adaptability to the kind of service in which he had employed them, and for which he regarded them as far better than the best white troops. "It would have been madness," he said, "to attempt with the bravest white troops what I have successfully accomplished with black ones." Their bearing "in battle," especially won his highest admiration. Then they exhibited, according to his account, a fiery energy beyond anything of which he had ever read, except of the French Zouaves. It required the strictest discipline to hold them in hand. They were ascending the river in steamers so constructed as to protect those within from the fire of small arms. In the first attack, and before Colonel Higginson could get "them all penned below," they crowded at the open ends of the steamers, loading and firing with unconceivable rapidity, and shouting to each other, "Never give it up." When collected into the hold they actually fought each other for places at the few portholes from which they could fire on the enemy. Their conduct generally on the expedition thoroughly convinced Colonel Higginson and all of his officers "that the key to the successful prosecution of this war lies in the unlimited employment of black troops."

CHAPTER VIII

At no time from the beginning of the war to the
spring of 1863 was the naval force of the South
Atlantic squadron deemed strong enough to encounter the land batteries defending Charleston harbor.
The duties of the fleet were therefore restricted so
far as concerned Charleston to the tedious and monotonous task of blockading the port, enlivened occasionally by a chase, sometimes succesful, of a
blockade runner.

More effectually to seal the port than the blockading fleet had been able to accomplish, an experiment was made to close it permanently by obstruct-
ing the channel. On December 20, 1861, the first
anniversary of the secession of South Carolina, a
fleet of seventeen old merchant vessels laden with
stone was anchored at regular and short intervals
in a line across the main channel, and having been
stripped were scuttled and sunk. On January 20
following another fleet of similar vessels was sunk
in like manner, four of them on the western end of
Rattlesnake Shoals, the others in the track of vessels entering Charleston harbor by Moffitt's Chan-

nel. The question naturally arose as to whether this method of blockading a port by destroying the entrance to it was admissible under the laws of nations, and it was thought it might lead to some international complications. But the experiment utterly failed. The irresistible waters of the Atlantic could not be stayed in their natural ebb and flow; the currents edging around the obstructions washed the sand from under them, speedily making as good a channel as ever by sinking the vessels deeper than had been intended; so deep that they offered no obstacle to ingress and egress.

After the failure of the assault on Secessionville and the abandonment by the Federal troops of the foothold they had secured on James Island in June, more than a year elapsed before any demonstration of note was made on Charleston by the land forces. In the meantime the operations against that city and its harbor were left to the navy, the land forces being in readiness to co-operate with it when occasion offered. Admiral DuPont remained in command of the South Atlantic squadron until July, 1863. General Beauregard had been assigned to the important and difficult command of the Department of South Carolina and Georgia, succeeding General Pemberton in that command on September 24, 1862.

Early in the morning of January 31, 1863, the blockading fleet off Charleston was surprised by a raid. There were two ironclad steamers or rams in Charleston harbor, which had been built at private shipyards in that city, the *Palmetto State* and *Chicora*. They were admirable vessels of their class, each armed with four heavy guns and well officered and manned. Captain John Rutledge commanded the *Palmetto State* and Captain John R. Tucker the *Chicora.* Commodore Duncan N. Ingraham commanded the station, with his flag on the *Palmetto State.* About a quarter past eleven o'clock on the night of the 30th the two steamers left their wharves and steamed slowly down to the bar, where they awaited the high tide to pass over. About four o'clock in the morning they crossed the bar and made directly for the blockading fleet. The *Palmetto State* went under full steam directly for the nearest vessel seen at anchor, which proved to be the United States steamer *Mercedita,* Captain Stillwagen commanding.

The Commodore ordered Captain Rutledge to strike with his prow and fire into her. As soon as the officer of the deck of the *Mercedita* saw the strange steamer approaching all hands were piped to quarters and the guns manned for action. Commander Stillwagen, who had just turned in, quickly sprang to his deck and, seeing the stranger close on him, hailed: "What steamer is that? Drop your anchor or you will be into us," and hearing the answer, "The Confederate steamer *Palmetto State,*" he immediately ordered, "Fire! fire!" These brief and hurried calls and answers, orders to quarters and to fire, were scarcely uttered when the *Palmetto State* struck the *Mercedita* on the quarter abaft the aftermost thirty-pounder, and at the same time fired a seven-inch shell, which crushed through her starboard side diagonally across, passing through the Normandy condenser and the steam drum, killing the gunner in his room and, exploding against the port side of the ship, tore a hole through it four or five feet square.

The vessel was instantly filled and enveloped with steam; outcries were heard that the shot had passed through both boilers, that the fires were extinguished by steam and water, that a number of men were killed and others scalded, and that the vessel was sinking rapidly. The Confederate commander called out: "Surrender or I will sink you. Do you surrender?" To which Captain Stillwagen replied: "I can make no resistance; my boiler is destroyed." "Then do you surrender?" "Yes," replied the captain of the *Mercedita,* and quickly sent Lieutenant Commander Abbott in a boat to the *Palmetto State* to make known the condition of his vessel and ascertain what the Confederate commander demanded. Lieutenant Abbott stated that he came in the name of Captain Stillwagen to surrender the United States steamer *Mercedita,* she being then in a sinking and perfectly defenseless condition, that she had a crew of 158, all told, that her boats were not large enough to save the crew, and had besides been lowered without the plugs being put in and had filled with water. He was informed that the officers and crew would be paroled, provided he would pledge his word of honor that neither he nor any of the officers or crew of the *Mercedita* would again take up arms against the Confederate States during the war, unless legally and regularly exchanged as prisoners of war. "Believing it to be the proper course

to pursue at the time, I consented," says Lieutenant
Abbott. The *Mercedita* did not fire a gun, the *Palmetto State* being so low in the water and so near
that the guns of the former could not be turned
on her.

In the meantime the *Chicora* fired into a schooner-
rigged propellor and it was believed set her on fire;
then engaged a large side-wheel steamer at close
quarters, firing three shots into her with telling effect,
which then put on all steam and ran off, escaping in
the dark. She then engaged a schooner-rigged propeller and the *Keystone State.* The latter was commanded by Captain Le Roy, United States Navy.
The first shot from the *Chicora* set her on fire in
her forward hold, when she kept off seaward to
gain time to extinguish the fire and prepare the ship
for action. About daylight she made for the *Chicora* for the purpose, if possible, of running her
down, exchanging shots with and "striking her repeatedly, but making no impression on her, while
every shot from her struck the *Keystone State* with
telling effect." About a quarter past six o'clock a
shell crashed through the *Keystone State's* port side
forward guard and destroyed the steam chimneys,
filling the forward part of the ship with steam. The
port boiler, emptied of its contents, so lightened her
on that side that the ship gave a heel to starboard
nearly down to the guard. The water from the
boiler, which was rapidly pouring through two
shot holes under water, produced the impression that
the ship was filling rapidly and sinking. A foot and
a half of water was reported in the hold.

To add to the embarrassment the fire, which it was supposed had been extinguished, broke out again, while the steam forward prevented the men from getting up ammunition, even if the ship and crew had been in condition to use it. The signal books and some arms were thrown overboard and all the boats were made ready for lowering. "The ram being so near," says Captain Le Roy, "the ship helpless and the men being slaughtered by almost every discharge of the enemy's guns, I ordered the colors to be hauled down; but finding the enemy were still firing upon us directed the colors to be rehoisted and returned fire from the after battery." In his official report Captain Le Roy makes no mention whatever of having struck his colors. His log-book, over his own signature, is much fuller in detail than his official report, and has been followed in the foregoing narrative.

Captain Tucker states in his report that when the *Keystone State* struck her colors she was completely at his mercy, as the *Chicora* had a raking position astern of her and distant about two hundred yards. A large number of the crew were seen rushing to the after part of the deck of the *Keystone State,* extending their arms towards the *Chicora* in an imploring manner. He immediately ceased firing upon her and ordered First Lieutenant Bier to man a boat and take charge of the prize and, if possible, to save her. If that were not possible, then to rescue the crew. While the lieutenant and men were in the act of manning the boat he discovered that the *Keystone State* was endeavoring to make her escape by working her starboard wheel, the other being disabled. Her colors being down, he at once started in pursuit and renewed the engagement, but owing to her superior steaming power she soon widened the distance to about two thousand yards, when she rehoisted her colors and commenced firing her rifle gun. She was soon taken in tow by the United States steamer *Memphis* and carried off to Port Royal.

The *Chicora* next engaged a brig and a bark-rigged propeller. Not having the requisite speed, she was unable to bring them to close quarters, but pursued them six or seven miles seaward. Toward the end of the engagement and in broad daylight she was engaged at long range with a large bark-rigged steamer. It was doubtless the *Housatonic,* as no other vessel appears to have been within range at that time. If so, the reports of the respective captains differ materially. Captain Tucker says that in spite of all his efforts he was unable to bring the steamer with which he was exchanging shots at long range to close quarters, owing to her superior steaming qualities.

The report of Captain Taylor, of the *Housatonic,* produces the impression that the *Chicora* was making for the harbor and desirous of avoiding an engagement with her adversary. She and the *Palmetto State* were heading toward the harbor, and the captain says he opened fire upon the ram as soon as he got within range (which was returned deliberately), and kept it up "as long as she remained within range. At no time did she (the *Chicora*) deviate from the course she was steering when we first saw her, except that she turned twice to bring her stern gun to bear on us." Admiral DuPont says: "The *Housatonic,* Captain Taylor, gave chase. . . . The Confederate vessels then passed to the northward, receiving the fire of our ships and took refuge in the swash channel behind the shoals." The Admiral was at Port Royal at the time and, of course, made his report on the faith of those made to him.

It is difficult to imagine why the commanders of the ironclads should have wished to avoid the combat and take shelter anywhere. They knew that all of the blockading vessels were of wood and most of them merchant steamers armed. They had the utmost confidence in the ability of the ironclads to destroy any and every one of those wooden steamers with which they might come into conflict, if the latter did not profit by superior speed to escape. They had gone into the midst of the fleet with no other purpose than to engage it. They had engaged several steamers successfully, crippling them greatly, while they (the ironclads) had received no injury, and there had not been a casualty in either vessel.

If, as Captain Taylor's report plainly implies, he was anxious to engage the ironclads with his wooden ship, why he did not do so seems inexplicable. The speed of the *Housatonic* was probably double that of the ironclads, which was but six or seven knots an hour. They had been in the midst of his fleet about four hours, and if from any cause he was prevented from following and engaging them at that time, he could have approached them at any time during the day, as they lay at anchor in four fathoms of water outside of the entrance to Beech Channel for about eight hours. They could not have gone inside sooner had Commodore Ingraham desired it, as there was not water enough on the bar to take them over except at high tide. An examination of the chart will show that while anchored in four fathoms they were very far beyond the range of any land battery.

Having disposed of the *Mercedita*, the *Palmetto State* stood to the northward and eastward and soon found another steamer getting under way, stood for her and fired several shots, but as the ram had to be fought in a circle to bring her different guns to bear the steamer was soon out of range. Just as day dawned a large steamer with a smaller one in company was seen under way on the starboard bow and standing to the southward under full steam. They opened their batteries on the *Chicora*, which was some distance astern of the *Palmetto State.* The latter turned and stood to the southward to support the *Chicora*, if necessary, but the two steamers kept on their course to the southward. The superior speed of the blockading steamers made pursuit of them hopeless. Commodore Ingraham therefore signaled Captain Tucker to come to anchor and lead the way to the entrance to Beech Channel. Captain Tucker accordingly stood in shore, "leaving," he says, "the partially crippled and fleeing enemy about seven miles clear of the bar, standing to the southward and eastward."

About half past eight o'clock the two Confederate

steamers were at anchor off Beech Channel in four fathoms water, where they remained until after four o'clock in the evening. They were not injured, had not even been struck, and there were no casualties. The Federal loss in the engagement was four killed and three wounded on the *Mercedita,* and on the *Keystone State* twenty killed and twenty wounded; total, forty-seven. The *Mercedita* had surrendered and the *Keystone State* struck her colors to escape destruction, thus virtually surrendering; but both escaped to Port Royal. The raid was over and soon the nearest of the blockading steamers was hull down off to sea, the masts visible to those on the Confederate steamers only with the aid of powerful glasses.

As soon as the result, or supposed result, of the raid on the blockading squadron was reported to General Beauregard, he telegraphed to the Adjutant General in Richmond that the Confederate States steam rams *Palmetto State* and *Chicora* had sunk the United States steamer *Mercedita* of the blockading squadron, that Captain Turner had set fire to one vessel, which struck her colors, and thought he sunk another. "Our loss and damage none. Enemy's whole fleet has disappeared north and south. I am going to proclaim the blockade raised." He and Commodore Ingraham united in issuing a proclamation setting forth that the Confederate States naval force had that morning attacked the United States blockading fleet off the harbor of Charleston, "and sunk, dispersed, or drove off and out of sight for the time the entire hostile fleet," and they formally declared the blockade raised by force of arms.

Copies of the proclamation were sent to the foreign consuls, and General Beauregard placed a steamer at their disposal to see for themselves that no blockade existed. The French and Spanish consuls accepted the invitation.[1] The Spanish consul, Señor Munez de Monceeda, replying to the offer, says: "Having gone out in company with the French consul and arrived at the point where the Confederate naval forces were, we discovered three steamers and a pilot boat returning. I must also mention that the British consul at this port manifested to me verbally, that some time subsequent to this naval combat not a single blockading vessel was in sight." That evening or night General Beauregard telegraphed the Adjutant General: "Some of the enemy's vessels have returned, but for several hours (three or four) none were in sight. Was blockade raised or not? What says the Attorney General? Shall I publish my proclamation, written meanwhile?"

The truth of the statements contained in the proclamation and made by the foreign consuls and the Charleston papers was vehemently denied by Captain William Rodgers Taylor and Commander J.

[1] The visit of the Spanish and French consuls was in the afternoon. The Charleston papers of about that date stated that the British consul, with the commander of the British war steamer *Petrel*, had previously gone five miles beyond the usual anchorage of the blockaders and could see nothing of them with their glasses.

H. Strong, James Madison Frailey, E. G. Parrott, Pend. G. Watmough and C. J. Van Alstine, all of them commanding vessels of the blockading fleet in an official joint certificate of February 10, 1863, addressed to Admiral DuPont. Their denial is expressed in very emphatic and harsh terms. It happened also that the One Hundred and Seventy-sixth Regiment Pennsylvania Militia was passing Charleston harbor that morning in the transport steamer *Cossack*, en route from Morehead City, N. C., to Port Royal, S. C. Colonel A. A. Leckler and Surgeon W. F. Funderburg, of the One Hundred and Seventy-sixth Pennsylvania, and Captain T. C. Newberry, commanding the *Cossack*, united in a letter of February 21, 1863, to Admiral DuPont, in which they deny the truth of the foregoing Confederate statements in terms quite as strong and harsh as did the naval officers. In the very early morning they heard some firing, but that was not unusual. They arrived off Charleston harbor about half past eight o'clock and found the blockading vessels at their usual stations at an estimated distance of from four to five miles from land. Some of the vessels were at anchor. They were in the midst of the fleet little less than an hour, and communicated with the officers, some of whom came on board their ship. The weather was a little hazy, but they saw land very clearly on both sides of the harbor. They denounce the statements from Confederate sources and the foreign consuls "as utterly false in every particular."

Statements so diametrically opposed when made

by men of high official and social positions ought to
admit of some satisfactory explanation without the
imputation of deliberate falsehood. It may be that
the denial was leveled mainly at the statements of
the sinking of any vessel and of raising the blockade,
but was made more sweeping and comprehensive
than the officers intended. It is true that the *Mercedita* had not been sunk, nor did the proclamation
state that it had been. It simply declared the blockade raised in a way recognized as valid under the
law of nations, namely, that the blockading fleet had
been "sunk, dispersed, or driven off and out of
sight" for the time by force of arms. A simple
statement of the facts as they are set forth in the
official reports of the Federal officers themselves
will show the grounds on which General Beauregard
and Commodore Ingraham based the statement.

Commodore Turner, of the United States steam
frigate *New Ironsides*, states that there were nine
blockading vessels lying off Charleston bar on the
morning of the attack. It would seem from the
statements of the Federal reports that the weather
was thick and hazy, so much so that the *Palmetto
State* was nearly upon the *Mercedita* before she was
seen by the officer of the deck of the latter, who was
on the alert. The *Mercedita* after being fired into
was surrendered with her crew, because, as her commander and executive officer stated, she was in a
sinking and perfectly helpless condition. When day
dawned she was nowhere to be seen, either by the
Confederate or Federal commanders. The latter,
Captain Taylor, was apprehensive that she had been

destroyed. It was therefore very natural that Commodore Ingraham and Captain Tucker should have believed she had sunk. She had, in fact, started about five o'clock for Port Royal, and when day dawned had been about an hour on that course and was out of sight.

The *Keystone State* had lost about a fourth of her crew and was so badly crippled that she struck her colors, and as soon as it was light was taken in tow by the *Memphis* and carried directly off to Port Royal. As soon as the raid was over, about eight o'clock, Captain Taylor dispatched the *Augusta*, Parrott commanding, to Port Royal to carry the news of the disaster to Admiral DuPont. Thus four of the nine blockading vessels of the fleet reached Port Royal after 3 o'clock P. M. that day. About 8 o'clock A. M. Captain Parrott reported to Captain Taylor what he had himself observed, that the United States steamers *Mercedita*, *Flag*, *Stellin*, and *Ottawa* could nowhere be seen, and search was made for them. Between 9 and 10 o'clock A. M., therefore, seven of the nine blockaders were out of sight, not only of the Confederate, but of the Federal commanders, leaving only two—the *Housatonic* and *Quaker City*—that could by any chance have been seen. Of these two Captain Taylor says: "The *Keystone State* was at this time in tow of the *Memphis* and distant (from him) two or three miles; the weather was unfavorable for signaling and I was steaming toward her when the *Quaker City* came up and expressed a desire to communicate. Commander Frailey reported having received a shell in his engine-room and required several articles to repair the damage." Between 8 and 9 o'clock A. M., therefore, the *Housatonic* was steaming southward to overtake two other vessels which were two or three miles off, when it fell in with the *Quaker City* in a crippled condition. It is not therefore marvelous that at about that time Captain Tucker, Confederate States Navy, should have reported that he left "the partially crippled and fleeing enemy about seven miles clear of the bar steaming to the southward and eastward."

Just where the *Housatonic* and *Quaker City* were when they came together between 8 and 9 o'clock A. M. does not appear; but it does appear from Captain Taylor's own statement that from day dawn to 3 o'clock P. M. the weather was so thick and hazy that at no time was the land distinctly visible, and that he did not start back to pick up his anchor, where he had left it when the raid began, until about three o'clock in the afternoon. The *Ottawa* did not appear on the scene during the engagement, and nothing is said of her in the official reports except that she was out of sight, but reported safe. She was probably in Stono River. Her station was nearer the Stono Inlet than the other vessels, and the morning of the 31st her commander sent word to Captain Taylor that the steamer *Isaac Smith* had been captured and that the *Commodore McDonough*, the only other gunboat in that river, was in danger. Early that morning a gunboat came into the river, steamed up it and shelled Legareville and then fell down the river, but returned in the evening and resumed fire. As the commander knew or had been informed that the gunboat *Mc-Donough* was in danger, and was himself so near at hand, it is reasonable to suppose that his was the gunboat that came into the river to assist the *Mc-Donough*. If so, she was clearly out of sight of the bar, leaving the *Housatonic* and *Quaker City* the only two of the nine blockading steamers mentioned by Commodore Turner as present that morning which could by any possibility have been seen.

Under all of these circumstances it is surely not wonderful or improbable that for three or four hours during that day the blockading fleet could not be seen by the Confederates who were near the bar, and that is all the proclamation stated as to its position. To everyone who knew General Beauregard and Commodore Ingraham their statement of facts will be received as absolutely true, and needs no argument to prove them. Whether the facts as they existed constituted a technical raising of the blockade is a question of law on which there may be honest difference of opinion.

Again, the six naval officers in their letter above mentioned say among other things: "These are the facts, and we do not hesitate to state that no vessel did come out beyond the bar after the return of the rams at between 7 and 8 A. M. to the cover of the forts. We believe the statement that any vessel came anywhere near the usual anchorage of any of the blockaders, or up to the bar after the withdrawal of the rams, to be deliberately and knowingly false." These statements, so unhesitatingly made and so harshly expressed, must in the case of at least three of those officers have been based on other evidence than their own observation. They could not have known personally whereof they spoke.

Two of them, Commanders Parrott and Watmough, started early in the morning for Port Royal and arrived there after 3 o'clock P. M. They therefore could not have had personal knowledge of what vessels came up to or over the Charleston harbor bar that day. Another, Commander Strong, was out of sight of his own commanding officer from day dawn until half-past ten o'clock, when he came up and brought news to Captain Taylor of the safety of the *Stellin* and *Ottowa*. The *Stellin* came up about eleven o'clock; her commander, Van Alstine, brought a message from Lieutenant Commander Whitney, of the *Ottowa*, that the United States steamer *Isaac Smith* had been captured in the Stono the previous evening and that the *Commodore McDonough* was in danger. Captain Strong was immediately sent into the Stono to assist the *McDonough*. The weather was so hazy all day that Captain Taylor could scarcely see land anywhere, and he was much nearer the bar than Captain Strong. How, then, could Captain Strong have spoken with such absolute certainty and from personal observation of what vessels were near the bar? How, indeed, could Captain Taylor himself, or the two other officers, Commanders Frailey and Van Alstine, have known what steamer came over the bar? Their vessels, according to the Confederate accounts, were hull down out to sea and only their masts could be seen by persons outside of the bar, and according to his own official report Taylor was so far out to sea and the weather so hazy that he could scarcely see land anywhere. It seems hopeless to attempt to reconcile the statements made by the landsmen of the One Hundred and Seventy-sixth Pennsylvania Regiment and the captain of the transport steamer *Cossack* with the concurrent official reports both Federal and Confederate.

The report brought to Captain Taylor on the morning of the 31st by Commander Van Alstine, of the capture the previous evening of a steamer in the Stono, proved true. The United States steamers *Commodore McDonough* and *Isaac Smith* had been in the habit for some time of running up and down the Stono reconnoitering and occasionally exchanging shots at long range with the land batteries. Generals Beauregard and Ripley planned an ambush which it was hoped would result in the capture of one, and perhaps both, of the steamers. The execution of the plan was intrusted to Lieutenant Colonel J. A. Yates, of the First South Carolina Artillery, a gentleman in every way admirably fitted for the successful performance of the duty.

On the night of January 29 two batteries of siege and field guns were placed in ambush near the right bank of the Stono, one of them at Trimble's place on John's Island, and one lower down at Legare Point Place. A third battery of three twenty-four pounder rifle guns was placed in ambush near Thomas Gimble's, higher up on the river and on the

James Island side. Major J. W. Brown, Second South Carolina; Major Charles Alston and Captain F. H. Harleston, of the South Carolina siege train, commanded the batteries on the John's Island side. The battery at Thomas Gimble's was commanded by Captain John H. Geary, Fifteenth South Carolina Heavy Artillery. Captain John C. Mitchell,[2] son of the Irish patriot, John Mitchell, commanded a battalion of two companies (Twentieth South Carolina Volunteers) of sharpshooters.

About 4 P. M. on the 30th the steamer *Isaac Smith,* Lieutenant Conover commanding, steamed up the Stono and anchored off Thomas Gimble's, about five hundred yards from Captain Geary's guns. The batteries had been so well screened from view that they were not seen by anyone on the steamer. Captain Geary waited about twenty minutes, hoping the crew would land, but discovering no signs of landing he opened, firing rapidly and with effect. The fire was quickly returned with shell, canister, and grape from the steamer, which at the same time slipped her anchor and started down the river. Then the upper battery on John's Island opened, and Lieutenant Connor discovered, as he says, that he was "entrapped," and that his only way of escape was to get below the batteries. To do that he would have to run the gauntlet of the land batteries and sharpshooters, fighting his way out.

[2] He was a handsome, gallant young Irish gentleman, and while commanding Fort Sumter in the summer of 1864 was killed on the parapet by a shell from Cumming's Point.

Owing to a bend in the river the steamer, while running more than a mile, was exposed to raking fires from batteries on both banks of the river, to which he could reply only with his pivot gun. As soon as he reached a part of the river where his broadsides could be brought to bear he opened with shell and grape at from two to four hundred yards' distance. But a shot through the steam chimney effectually stopped the engine, and with but little tide and no wind to carry him down the river and his boats riddled with shots he was entirely at the mercy of the enemy. Exposed to the concentrated fire from the batteries on both sides and the rifles of Captain Mitchell's sharpshooters, "the shot tearing through the vessel in every direction and with no hope of being able to silence such a fire," Lieutenant Conover thought it his duty to surrender, and accordingly hauled down his colors and ran up the white flag.

"Had it not been for the wounded men," he says, "with which the berth deck was covered, I might have blown up or sunk the ship, letting the crew take the chance of getting on shore by swimming; but under the circumstances I had no alternative left me." The steamer and entire crew, consisting of 11 officers and 108 men, were surrendered. The loss on the steamer was 9 killed and 16 wounded, among the latter the lieutenant commanding. The Confederate loss was 1 man mortally wounded and 1 gun disabled. The steamer was armed with one 30-pounder Parrot rifle and eight 8-inch columbiads.

She was but little injured, was soon repaired, and passed into the Confederate service under the name of the *Stono*.

Commander Bacon, of the *McDonough*, which was in Stono Inlet, hearing the firing up the river, got under way and steamed up to assist the *Smith*, but soon discovered the white flag flying over her and her crew in boats going ashore as prisoners. He continued to move on up with the intention of towing her off or blowing her up. Before getting sufficiently near to accomplish anything the guns at Point Place, which had taken no part in the fire on the *Smith*, and whose presence then was unknown, opened on the *McDonough* and were followed quickly by other guns. The steamer moved back down the river, returning the fire of the land batteries and keeping in motion to prevent her range being ascertained until dark, when she was beyond effective range. Commander Bacon then turned his guns upon the pretty little town of Legareville, throwing shells into it, "in the hope," he says, "of setting fire to the place."

CHAPTER IX

Among the United States war vessels which were
destroyed or partially destroyed by the Federal officers on the eve of their evacuation of Norfolk and
the Gosport Navy Yard, April 20, 1861, was the
United States steam frigate *Merrimac,* which was
burned to her copper line and berth-deck, scuttled,
and sunk. Subsequently she was raised by Confederate naval officers, reconstructed on a novel model,
encased in iron plates, armed with heavy guns and
an iron prow, and soon became famous as the Confederate States steam ram *Merrimac.* The report
went abroad that she was invulnerable to any guns
then in use, and could readily overcome and destroy
any vessels then in the navy with which she might
come in collision.

The knowledge of the existence of this novel
engine of war caused no little apprehension in the
North, which was greatly heightened by the ease
with which she and her consorts sunk the United
States ship *Cumberland* and destroyed the *Congress*

in Hampton Roads on March 8, 1862. Excitable
and imaginative people even apprehended that New
York city and Philadelphia would soon be under the
fire of her guns. It became therefore a grave question how the steam ram could be destroyed.

To that end an ironclad steamer designed by Captain John Ericsson on a new model was speedily constructed, and was the first of the class of war vessels
since known as monitors. Seven of them were hastily
constructed, armed with heavier guns than ever
before used, and sent to Port Royal, S. C., to operate against Charleston. Early in January, 1863,
several of them were on their way to Port Royal.
(The original *Monitor* foundered at sea off Cape
Hatteras, and two others, the *Montauk* and *Passaic*,
narrowly escaped the same fate.)

While awaiting the arrival of the full number,
Admiral DuPont deemed it prudent to test the power
of those that had arrived, and selected as the object
on which to make the experiment Fort McAlister,
an earthwork at Genesis Point, on the Ogeechee
River, near Savannah, and if possible destroy or capture it. On January 27, and again on February 1,
the *Montauk*, aided by several other less formidable
vessels, engaged the fort. On March 3 the *Montauk*, having been joined by three other monitors, the
Passaic, *Patapsco*, and *Nahant*, and aided by other
vessels, again engaged the earthwork. The attack
and defense of Fort McAlister do not come within
the proposed limits of this narration. Suffice it to say
that after a bombardment of eight hours, in which

the fire of the fort was directed exclusively on the *Passaic,* the monitors withdrew.

No injury was done to the fort that could not readily be repaired during the night, says Admiral Ammen, who commanded the *Patapsco.* The gunboats and mortar schooners, which fired at the distance of about four hundred yards, did neither good nor harm. On March 6 the monitors were taken in tow to Port Royal. The *Passaic* had been so damaged in the bombardment that she required three weeks of repairs, to be put in serviceable condition again.

By April 1 the whole monitor fleet was in North Edisto Inlet—an admirable harbor, about twenty miles from Charleston bar—and as thoroughly provided as they could be for the attack on Charleston. Such a fleet had never before been seen. Its capacity for destruction and resistance was unknown. In the North it was looked to with confidence, hope, and expectation for the accomplishment of an object so ardently desired,—the reduction of Charleston,— while in the South it unquestionably excited grave apprehension.

Major General Hunter, commanding the Department of the South, with an aggregate land force present of a little over twenty-three thousand men, moved up a large part of his force and occupied Folly and Seabrook's islands and other points on or near the Stono, and prepared to follow up the expected success of the fleet and occupy Charleston.

The concentration of such formidable land and

naval forces at Port Royal, Hilton Head, and North
Edisto had warned General Beauregard, then commanding the Department of South Carolina and
Georgia, that the long expected attack on Charleston
was immediately impending, and he prepared to meet
it. The troops nearest the city were distributed as
seemed best to meet the coming storm, and arrangements made to draw reinforcements quickly, if required, from other points in his department.

The first military district of the department, which
embraced the defenses of Charleston, was commanded by Brigadier General Roswell S. Ripley, an
officer of distinguished ability, great energy, and
fertile in resource; no more accomplished artillery
officer could have been found in either army. He
was especially charged with the defenses of the
harbor, and the completeness of the preparations
was in a great measure due to his skill and energy.
Brigadier General James H. Trapier commanded
the second subdivision of the district, which embraced Sullivan's Island. The defensive works on
that island—Fort Moultrie and Batteries Beauregard and Bee—were under the general direction of
Colonel Lawrence M. Keitt.

Fort Sumter, the chief object of attack, was commanded by Colonel Alfred Rhett, of the First South
Carolina Regular Artillery, and was garrisoned by
seven companies of that regiment. Lieutenant Colonel J. A. Yates and Major Ormsby Blanding, of the
same regiment, had general charge, the first of the
barbette, the latter of the casemate batteries.

Brigadier General S. R. Gist commanded the first

subdivision of the district, which embraced James' Island and St. Andrew's. It was known that General Hunter had concentrated the mass of his force on Folly Island and its vicinity, and it was supposed would co-operate with the fleet by an attack either on James or Morris Island. The responsible duty of meeting the enemy in that quarter was confided to General Gist.

Colonel R. F. Graham commanded the small force on Morris Island, on which were the very important works, Batteries Gregg and Wagner.

On the morning of April 5 Admiral DuPont, on his flagship, the *New Ironsides,* having joined the "ironclads," as they were generally called, at South Edisto, the whole fleet steamed toward Charleston harbor, the monitors in tow of suitable steamers. That evening, having sounded and buoyed the bar of the main channel, the *Keokuk,* the *Patapsco,* and *Kaatskill* passed the bar and anchored within. The next morning the Admiral, his flag flying on the *New Ironsides,* crossed the bar, followed by the other ironclads. It was his intention to proceed the same day to Charleston, attacking Fort Sumter on the way, but the weather was unfavorable and the pilots refused to proceed further.

At midday on the 7th signal was made for the whole fleet to move forward to the attack. The order of battle was "line ahead," the vessels moving in the following order: The *Weehawken,* Captain John Rodgers; the *Passaic,* Captain Percival Drayton; the *Montauk,* Captain John L. Worden; the *Patapsco,* Commander Daniel Ammen; the *New*

Ironsides (flagship), Commodore Thomas Turner; the *Kaatskill*, Commander George W. Rodgers; the *Nantucket*, Commander Donald McN. Fairfax; the *Nahant*, Commander John Downs, and the *Keokuk*, Commander A. C. Rhind.

The *New Ironsides* carried fourteen 11-inch guns and two 150-pounder Parrott rifles; the *Patapsco*, one 15-inch and one 150-pounder Parrot rifle. The *Keokuk*, two 11-inch guns; the others one 15-inch and one 11-inch gun each.

Commanders were ordered to pass the Morris Island batteries, Wagner and Gregg, without returning their fire, unless specially signaled to do so by the Admiral. They were directed to take positions to the north and west of Sumter, within about eight hundred yards, and open, firing low with great care, and aiming at the center embrasures. The Admiral's order of battle adds: "After the reduction of Fort Sumter it is probable that the next point of attack will be the batteries on Morris Island." A squadron of vessels, consisting of the *Canandaigua*, *Housatonic*, *Huron*, *Unadilla*, and *Wissahickon*, Captain J. F. Green commanding, was held in reserve outside the bar and near the entrance buoy, in readiness to support the ironclads in the proposed attack on the Morris Island batteries.

The *Weehawken* was handicapped and incumbered by a raft attached to its bow to explode torpedoes.[1] In weighing anchor her chain became en-

---

[1] It was called the "Devil" and was cut adrift and floated ashore on Morris Island.

tangled in the grapnels of the raft, delaying the line nearly two hours. About 1:15 the whole fleet was under way, but the raft attached to the *Weehawken* delayed her and the ironclads that were following, causing wild steering along the whole line; the monitors "sheering every way" when their engines stopped, so that it was impossible to preserve the ordered interval of one hundred yards between the vessels.

The weather was as calm and the water as smooth as could have been desired for naval firing. Reports had gone abroad of the extent of the obstructions and number of torpedoes in the harbor. While moving into action a number of buoys were observed, unpleasantly suggestive of the presence of torpedoes, one of which exploded near the *Weehawken,* lifting her somewhat, but without disabling her.

Just before the leading vessel came within range the long roll was beat in Fort Sumter, "the garrison, regimental and palmetto flags were hoisted and saluted by thirteen guns, the band playing the national air, 'Dixie.' " A few minutes before 3 o'clock P. M., the leading monitor having approached to within about two thousand yards of Fort Moultrie, the action was opened by a shot from that fort, fired by its commander, Colonel William Butler. Three minutes later the leading monitor, when about fifteen hundred yards from Sumter, fired two guns simultaneously. Then Sumter opened, firing by battery. The action became general and for more than two hours nearly a hundred guns on land and water, many of them of the heaviest caliber yet ever used, were in rapid action.

It was a calm and balmy day in spring—the season of greatest natural beauty and luxuriance in that mild region. It was the season at which Charleston had been wont to present its most attractive phase, when the wealthy planters and their families had not yet been driven by the heat from their city houses and when the hotels were most crowded with visitors from the North. In strong contrast to the picture of tranquil pleasure and enjoyment, in a mild, delicious climate, which the city had formerly presented at this season, was the scene of strained excitement and anxiety on this day of the attack on the harbor defenses of Charleston. From every point of view in the city the eyes of the many thousands of spectators were riveted on the grand and imposing spectacle. The church steeples, roofs, windows, and piazzas of houses on the "Battery" were crowded with eager, breathless witnesses of this bombardment, the precursor of a siege which was to arouse in the people there assembled and those whom they represented every high and patriotic hope, every reserve of courage and endurance, the sublimest exercise of patience and submission.

From the blockading fleet and transports off the bar this trial of strength and endurance between forts and ships, the latter brought to the highest point of precision and destructive power, was witnessed by other anxious spectators, who confidently anticipated a brilliant victory for the fleet, with feelings scarcely less intense than those of the people in the city who fully realized the importance to them of the events which hung upon the issue.

Through the thunder of artillery ran the heavy thud of the huge shells as they pounded the brick walls of Sumter and the sharp metallic ring and crash of the shot and shells as they struck the iron turrets and casings of the monitors, tearing away the iron plates, crashing through the sides and decks, or shivering into fragments by the concussion and falling then in showers about the deck or into the water.

The ironclads came into action in succession, and though the engagement lasted about two hours and twenty minutes, from thirty to forty-five minutes' exposure to the fire of the forts and batteries sufficed to put the vessels *hors de combat.*

The *Weehawken* fired twenty-six shots and was struck fifty-three times. A part of her side armor was so shattered that it hung in splintered fragments, which could be pulled off with the hand, thus exposing the woodwork. Her deck was pierced, making a hole through which the water poured, and her turret was so shaken by the pounding to which it was subjected that it revolved with difficulty, thus greatly retarding her fire.

The *Passaic,* Captain Percival Drayton, was even more roughly handled than the *Weehawken.* She succeeded in firing only thirteen shots and was struck thirty-five times. At the fourth discharge of her 11-inch gun the turret was struck twice in quick succession, bulging in its plates and beams and forcing together the rails on which the gun-carriage worked, rendering the gun wholly useless for the remainder of the action. An instant later the turret was so jammed that it could not be moved, thus effectually ending its fire. The turret was again struck by a heavy rifle shot, which shattered all of the eleven plates on the upper edge, then glancing upward struck the pilot house with such force as to mash it in, bend it over, open the plates and press them out and, lifting the top, exposing the inside to such a degree that another shot would, it was thought, knock the top entirely off. Under the terrific fire to which his vessel was exposed Captain Drayton could not examine it to ascertain the extent of the injury. He could not fire a shot, and signaled the Admiral for permission to withdraw; but receiving no answer, he did not stand on the order of his going, but went at once out of range. He could not discover then, nor the next morning when he had a good view of the exposed face of the fort, that it was in the least injured, and he was satisfied that under the circumstances then existing, "the monitors were no match for the forts."

The *Montauk* suffered less than her predecessors, but the brief engagement convinced her commander, Captain Worden, "that Charleston cannot be taken by the naval force now present, and that had the attack continued it could not have failed to result in disaster."

The *Patapsco* opened fire on Sumter with her 150-pounder rifle at fifteen hundred yards, and with her 15-inch gun at twelve hundred yards. At the fifth discharge the 150-pounder was disabled for the re-

mainder of the action.   The commanders of the
leading vessels, apprehending entanglement by drift-
ing within the rope obstructions which could be seen
ahead, turned their prows seaward.   The *Patapsco,*
endeavoring to follow their lead, refused to obey her
helm, and was detained sufficiently long to receive the
concentrated fire of Sumter and the Sullivan Island
batteries.   She was struck forty-seven times and her
turret was so battered as to prevent or greatly retard
its turning, thus rendering her only remaining gun
next to useless, when she retired out of range.

The turning back of the four leading monitors
and their moving seaward threw the line into much
confusion, the vessels becoming somewhat entangled,
so much so that the flagship came into collision with
two of the monitors and was obliged to anchor twice
to prevent running ashore.   She could not fire on
Fort Sumter without great risk of firing into the
monitors, but was detained at the distance of about
a mile from Fort Sumter, subjected to a heavy fire,
all the more galling because it could not be returned.
She only fired eight shots at Fort Moultrie.

The Confederate account says she was struck
sixty-three times at the distance of between seventeen hundred and eighteen hundred yards, and then
moved to the distance of two thousand yards—out of
effective range.   She was less injured than the monitors, probably because she was, for want of sufficient
depth of water, at a greater distance than they.   One
of her port shutters was shot away and Commander
Turner, in his official report to the Admiral, says:

"My impression is, had you been able to get this

ship into close position, where her broadsides would have been brought to bear, that not one port shutter would have been left under the fire of such enormous projectiles as were thrown from the enemy's works multiplied on every side of us."

For several minutes she was in greater peril than any on board perhaps knew. She was directly over a torpedo, which from some unknown cause failed to explode.

Finding his own ship blocking the way, the Admiral signaled: "Disregard the movements of the Commander-in-Chief"; and the rear vessels passed ahead, and coming under fire shared substantially the same fate as those that preceded them. Commander Fairfax, of the *Nantucket,* says that having approached close to the obstructions thrown across the channel he opened fire on Sumter:

"We were then under the fire of three forts, and most terrible was it for forty-five or fifty minutes. Our fire was very slow, necessarily, and not half so observable upon the walls of the forts as the rain of the rifle shots and heavy shells was upon this vessel. . . . Certainly their [the Confederate] firing was excellent throughout; fortunately, it was directed to some half dozen ironclads at once. . . . Our vessels could not long have withstood the concentrated fire of the enemy's batteries. . . . I must say that I am disappointed beyond measure at this experiment of monitors overcoming strong forts. It was a fair trial."

His fifteen-inch gun fired but three shots when it

was disabled for the remainder of the action and his eleven-inch rifle fired twelve times.

Commander Downs gives a lamentable account of the experience of his monitor, the *Nahant,* under a fire "of one hundred guns," as he erroneously supposed, which he describes as terrific, and he believed almost unprecedented. The blows from heavy shot very soon so jammed the turret that it could not be turned, which effectually stopped his fire. The concussion of a heavy shot on the pilot house forced off on the inside a piece of iron weighing seventy-eight pounds, and drove it with such violence that in its course to the other side it came in contact with the steering-gear, bending and disarranging it so that it could not be worked.

Bolt-heads were forced off and driven in showers about the pilot house and turret, one of them mortally wounding the quartermaster, Edward Cobb, and others knocking the pilot, Mr. Sofield, senseless, leaving the commander himself alone in the pilot house. His vessel was struck thirty-six times, the iron plating was broken in several places, and in some stripped from the wood backing, which was broken. He describes the effects of the shot more minutely than the other commanders, to draw attention to the weak points of the monitors for the benefit of future builders of such vessels. After repeated and futile efforts to train his guns on the fort and renew the action, he abandoned the effort and withdrew.

The *Keokuk* was the rear vessel of the line. Her

commander, A. C. Rhind, becoming impatient of the
long delay, passed not only the *Ironsides*, but the
vessels ahead of him and, defiantly directing his prow
toward Sumter, approached nearer than any other
vessel had done, firing as he advanced, and drawing
on the *Keokuk* the concentrated fire of Sumter,
Moultrie, Bee, and the battery on Cumming's Point.
But he was permitted to fire only three shots.   Commander Rhind's daring gallantry in carrying his vessel into action was equaled only by the frankness and
brevity with which he officially reported the result.
He says:

"The position taken by the *Keokuk* was maintained for about thirty minutes, during which period
she was struck ninety times in the hull and turrets.
Nineteen shots pierced through at and just below
the water line.   The turrets were pierced in many
places; one of the forward port shutters shot away;
in short, the vessel was completely riddled.   Finding
it impossible to keep her afloat many minutes more
under such an extraordinary fire, during which rifle
projectiles of every species and the largest caliber,
as also hot shot, were poured into us, I reluctantly
withdrew from action at 4:40 P. M., with the gun-
carriage of the forward turret disabled and so many
of the crews of the after gun wounded as to prevent
a possibility of remaining under fire.   I succeeded
in getting the *Keokuk* to an anchor out of range of
fire and kept her afloat during the night in the smooth
water, though the water was pouring into her in
many places."

In the morning the water becoming a little ruffled,

she sank, leaving only her smoke-stack out to show her position. Her crew, with the killed and wounded, were taken off.

About half-past four Admiral DuPont signaled the fleet to withdraw, intending to renew the attack the next day. By five o'clock the monitors were under way, following the flagship seaward, and soon anchored out of range, but within the bar, the fire of the forts gradually ceasing as the fleet receded.

The fire of the fleet had been directed mainly against Fort Sumter, but little attention being given to the other batteries. The flagstaff of Fort Moultrie was shot down, killing in its fall Private Lusby, of the First South Carolina Infantry. There was no other casualty on Sullivan's Island. When the flagstaff fell, Captains Wigg and Wardlaw and Lieutenants King and Calhoun quickly sprang to the top of a traverse and on the parapet and displayed the regimental, garrison, and battle flags in conspicuous positions.

Fort Sumter, though not seriously damaged, was more injured than the Federals seem to have thought, but not as much as might have been expected from the impact on brick walls of the heaviest shot ever yet used in war. The walls were struck by about thirty-six of those heavy shot.[2] Two 15-inch shells

[2]Admiral Ammen, in his book, says the fort was struck fifty-five times, and it appears from the report of the Confederate engineer who examined the fort immediately after the action that there were that number of marks or scars on the walls, but he says that many of those scars were made by fragments of shells that exploded in front of the walls.

penetrated the eastern face near an embrasure of the second tier, one exploding in the casemate, the other in the middle of the fort. One 11-inch shot also penetrated the wall. The carriage of a 10-inch columbiad was demolished and a 42-pounder was dismounted, both of which were promptly remounted and made ready for action. Five men were wounded by fragments of masonry and wood in Fort Sumter; three were killed and five wounded in Fort Wagner by an accidental explosion of an ammunition chest.

The Confederates had sixty-nine guns of various caliber in action, but only forty-one of them (exclusive of mortars) were above the caliber of thirty-two pounders. The armament of the fleet was thirty-two guns (eight of which, it seems, were not fired), of 8-, 11-, and 18-inch caliber, which at a single discharge could throw nearly as great a weight of metal as could the land batteries.

The Confederates fired in all 2229 shots and consumed 21,093 pounds of powder. The fleet fired 142 (the Confederates say 151) shots and consumed nearly 5000 pounds of powder. The two combined fired upon an average of seventeen shots, varying in weight from 30 to 400 pounds (or about 1300 pounds of iron), and consumed about 185 pounds of powder per minute, during 140 consecutive minutes, the heaviest fire ever yet delivered in so brief a bombardment.

The Confederate fire seems to have been much more accurate than the Federal. About an equal proportion of the shots fired on each side struck the objects at which they were aimed, but there was a very wide difference in the sizes of those objects. A monitor afloat is "in appearance not inaptly likened to a cheese box on a plank," the "plank" representing the deck and the "cheese box" the revolving turret in which are the guns. Its apparent length is 200 feet and beam 45 feet. The hull, however, is but 159 feet in length. The turret is 21 feet and 10 inches in diameter and 9 feet high. It is surmounted by a pilot house 9 feet 4 inches in diameter and 7 feet high. From bow to stern the deck varies from 2½ to 1½ feet above the water. An exceedingly small part, therefore, of the hull was exposed above water to fire. They were in motion also during the action.

Such an object in motion presented but a small mark at which to fire at the distance of from one thousand to fifteen hundred yards. Fort Sumter on the contrary was a very large and stationary object, presenting fronts of three tiers of guns at which to aim. The accuracy of the Confederate fire was due in a great measure to an ingenious contrivance of Lieutenant Colonel Yates, which enabled five men to hold the heaviest guns trained on the ironclads when in motion.

The little damage that Fort Sumter suffered was promptly repaired during the night and the weak points in the walls which the fire had disclosed were reinforced by sand-bags. The Confederates confidently expected the engagement to be renewed the next day, and the forts and batteries were as well prepared to receive an attack on the morning of the 8th as they had been on the morning of the 7th.

But it was not renewed. "The enemy was beaten," says General Ripley, "before their adversaries thought the action had well commenced."

During the evening of the 7th the commanders of the ironclads went on board the flagship and verbally reported to the Admiral the incidents of the engagement and the condition of their respective vessels. Their reports decided him not to renew the attack, and he promptly forwarded to the Secretary of the Navy a dispatch, in which he says:

"I yesterday moved up with eight ironclads and this ship and attacked Fort Sumter, intending to pass it and commence action on its northwest face, in accordance with my order of battle. The heavy fire received from it and Fort Moultrie and the nature of the obstructions compelled the attack from the outside. It was fierce and obstinate, and the gallantry of the officers and men of the vessels engaged was conspicuous. This vessel could not be brought into such close action as I endeavored to get her. Owing to the narrow channel and rapid current she became partly unmanageable, and was twice forced to anchor to prevent her going ashore, once owing to her having come into collison with two of the monitors. She could not get nearer than one thousand yards. Owing to the condition of the tide and an unavoidable accident, I had been compelled to delay action until in the afternoon, and toward evening, finding no impression made upon the fort, I made a signal to withdraw the ships, intending to renew the attack this morning.

"But the commanders of the monitors came on

board and reported verbally the injuries of their vessels, when without hesitation or consultation (for I never hold councils of war) I determined not to renew the attack, for in my judgment it would have converted a failure into a disaster, and I will only add that Charleston cannot be taken by a purely naval attack, and the army could give me no co-operation."

In reply to a complimentary letter from General Hunter, who had witnessed the action in a transport steamer, the Admiral says:

"I feel very comfortable, General, for the reason that a merciful Providence permitted me to have a failure, instead of a disaster."

Admiral Ammen, who commanded the *Patapsco*, says in his recently published book, "The Atlantic Coast":

"The result of the attack was mortifying to all of the officers and men engaged in it. Had any loss of life been regarded as likely to render another attempt successful, there would have been few indeed who would not have desired it. The opinion before the attack was general, and was fully shared in by the writer, that whatever might be the loss in men and vessels blown up by torpedoes or otherwise destroyed (and such losses were supposed probable), at all events Fort Sumter would be reduced to a pile of ruins before the sun went down."

General Beauregard had confidently expected every man of his command to do his duty, and he was not disappointed, for their hearts were thoroughly in their work. Confederate and Federal officers alike bear testimony to the accuracy of the Confederate fire, while the monitors themselves bore mute but more expressive evidence of its effects.

All that professional skill and gallantry could do had been done by the officers and crews of the vessels to achieve success. They had fought the united ironclads to their utmost capacity. The result had proved that these novel engines of naval warfare on which such high hopes were built had not materially changed the military relations between forts and ships. It had also given another striking proof of the fallacy of the belief that, *caeteris paribus,* ships can reduce forts. Just two years previously, less one week, Confederate land batteries had opened fire on Fort Sumter, newly constructed by United States engineers, at greater distance than that which the monitors had attacked, and with greatly inferior guns had compelled its surrender. A few months later Federal land batteries on Morris Island, at more than double the monitors' distance, had demolished the exposed walls of Fort Sumter.

This attack also illustrated what was conspicuous throughout the war, the great difference in the relative numbers of killed and wounded in battles on land and those between forts and ships. In this engagement between the Federal ironclad fleet and the forts and batteries at the entrance to Charleston, the casualties on the Confederate side were one killed and five wounded. On the Federal, one killed and twenty wounded. Little less than a year before in a battle on James' Island in sight of Fort Sumter nearly nine hundred men had been killed or wounded in less than half an hour.

The fleet remained within the bar but out of range, repairing and refitting, until high tide on the evening of the 12th, when it passed out, the *New Ironsides* taking her place with the blockading fleet, and the monitors were towed southward to Port Royal for repairs, leaving only the *Keokuk* sunk with her smokestack out of water marking her position. In a few days the Confederates dived into her and lifted out her heavy guns, flags, swords, and smaller articles. Her guns were soon mounted in the Confederate batteries.

When the news of the failure reached Washington President Lincoln dispatched Admiral DuPont:

EXECUTIVE MANSION, April 13, 1863.

Hold your position inside the bar near Charleston, or, if you have left it, return to it and hold it until further orders. Do not allow the enemy to erect new batteries or defenses on Morris Island. If he has begun it, drive him out. I do not herein order you to renew the general attack. That is to depend on your discretion or further orders.

A. LINCOLN.

The following day, April 14, he dispatched to the Admiral and General Hunter jointly:

This is intended to clear up any inconsistency between the recent order to continue operations before Charleston and the former one to remove to another point in a certain contingency. No censure upon you, or either of you, is intended; we still hope by cordial and judicious co-operation you can take the batteries on Morris Island and Sullivan's Island and Fort Sumter. But whether you can or not, we wish the demon-

stration kept up for a time for a collateral and very important
object; we wish the attempt to be a real one (though not a
desperate one) if it affords any considerable chance of success.
But if prosecuted for a demonstration only, this must not be
made public, or the whole effect will be lost.   Once again
before Charleston, do not leave till further orders from here.
Of course this is not intended to force you to leave unduly
exposed Hilton Head or other near points in your charge.

A. LINCOLN.

Replying through the Navy Department, the Admiral assured the Secretary that he would urge forward the repairs of the serious injuries sustained by
the monitors and return within the bar as soon as
possible; he thought, however, that the move would
be attended with great risk to the monitors from
gales and the fire of the enemy's batteries, which
"they could neither silence nor prevent the erection
of new ones." He would, of course, obey with fidelity
all orders he might receive, even when entirely at
variance with his own judgment, such as the order
to reoccupy the unsafe anchorage off Morris Island,
"and an intimation that a renewal of the attack on
Charleston may be ordered, which in my judgment
would be attended with disastrous results, involving
the loss of this coast." He was painfully struck by
the tenor and tone of the President's orders, which,
he thought, implied censure, and requested the Secretary not to hesitate to relieve him by an officer who
might be thought "more able to execute that service
in which I have had the misfortune to fail--the capture of Charleston."

In Washington, and in the North generally, it
had been confidently believed that the attack would

result in the fall of Charleston. So confident was the Navy Department of a successful result, that on the 2d of April orders were issued and dispatched to Admiral DuPont to send a number of the ironclads, which the fall of Charleston would render available, to the Gulf of Mexico for service in that quarter and in the Mississippi. The failure was a grievous disappointment in the North, while in the South the vague but serious apprehension of danger from the ironclads was dispelled, and in Charleston especially it was felt that the city had nothing to apprehend from the fleet alone.

Of course the failure was sharply criticised in the Northern press. Whoever relies on the newspapers of the period for correct information in regard to the battles of that war will inevitably be led into grave errors. In regard to this naval attack, some of the papers severely censured the Administration for ordering or permitting it without providing ample means to insure success, and the causes of the failure were fully explained. The ironclads, it was said, while moving up to the attack had become entangled in the rope obstructions which were well known to be in the channel and, while so hampered, had been exposed to the fire of three hundred guns, many of them supplied from England and of the heaviest caliber ever used in war, and at short range, in some instances three hundred yards.

The Secretary of State, Mr. Seward, seems to have obtained some of his information on the subject from the newspapers rather than from the official reports. In a printed circular letter signed by him and addressed to the diplomatic agents of the government abroad he says:

"An attack by the fleet on the 7th of April last upon the forts and batteries which defend the harbor of Charleston failed, because the rope obstructions in the channel fouled the screws of the ironclads and compelled them to return, after passing through the fire of the batteries. These bore the fire of the forts, although some defects of construction were revealed by the injuries they received. The crews passed through the unexampled cannonade with singular impunity. Not a life was lost on board a monitor."

None of the ironclads approached the rope obstructions nearer than six hundred yards, except the *Keokuk*, which, after being disabled, drifted within about three hundred yards of them before she could be got under way again. The rope obstructions were therefore not encountered by any of the vessels. They had not passed through the fire of the forts, for some of the heaviest batteries had not been brought into action. The *Keokuk*, as has been stated, was not nearer Fort Sumter than nine hundred yards, and none of the other vessels was so near any of the forts or the batteries. The ranges varied from nine hundred to about two thousand yards.

Instead of three hundred, there were but seventy-six Confederate guns of all kinds in action. Some of these were mortars, the fire of which on so small a target as a monitor and at such long range is so inaccurate as to be practically ineffective. Of the other guns only forty-one were above the caliber of 32-pounders, and guns of this latter caliber were of little avail against the ironclads. The most effective fire was from ten 10-inch and nineteen 8-inch columbiads, three 9-inch Dahlgrens and two 7-inch Brook guns, and they were American, not English guns. Judging by the effects of the fire from the guns actually engaged, and at such long range, it is hardly extravagant to suppose that if, during the two hours and twenty-five minutes the action lasted, the ironclads had been exposed to the fire of three hundred guns, at distances of from three to nine hundred yards, every one of them would have been sunk or irreparably disabled.

General Hunter had held his troops on Folly, Cole's, and Seabrook's islands in readiness to follow up the expected naval success. On the morning after the attack all was in readiness to cross Lighthouse Inlet to Morris Island "where," says the General, "once established, the fall of Sumter would have been as certain as the demonstration of a problem in mathematics." But the active co-operation of the navy was deemed necessary to insure the success of the movement. The crossing, however, was suspended because of the announcement of the Admiral that he had resolved to retire. The General sent an officer of his staff to represent to the Admiral his readiness to make the movement, the great importance of making it promptly when the enemy was unprepared to dispute it successfully, and to urge him to co-operate actively with the fire of his fleet. But to all of these considerations, says the General, "earnestly and elaborately urged, the Admiral's answer was that he 'would not fire another shot.'"

The intended movement was therefore abandoned or indefinitely suspended. The land as well as the naval expedition had come to naught and further movements for the capture of Charleston were deferred.[8]

[8]In this narrative I have followed substantially the official reports of the commanders of the ironclads, especially on all points of which their knowledge may reasonably be supposed more accurate than that of the Confederate officers. The only material differences between the Federal and Confederate reports are as to the distances of the vessels from the forts, batteries, and obstructions. As to them, I have followed the Confederate reports, because the officers making them had been on duty in the harbor defenses for many months—some of them for two years. They had made the harbor a military study, had placed obstructions, planted torpedoes, anchored buoys, and carefully measured the distances that it was desirable to know. They therefore of necessity had more accurate knowledge on those points than the naval officers could have gathered in the brief period of the action, when they were in strange waters, under a terrific fire, their attention riveted to the work in hand, with such limited view of the harbor as they could catch through the small circular holes in the pilot-houses and the two port-holes in the revolving turrets, while the smoke was so dense that as Commodore Turner says, often he could not see distinctly fifty yards ahead. Under such circumstances they could scarcely be expected to judge distances accurately. Colonel Rhett, the commander of Sumter, had waited deliberately until the leading monitor had reached a buoy the distance of which was well known, and on which his guns were trained, before opening fire. Both Colonel Rhett and his adjutant made careful observations during the whole action.

CHAPTER X

In order to reap all the advantages the combined Federal land and naval forces could gain on the South Atlantic coast, it was obviously necessary that there should be very earnest and hearty co-operation between those arms of service, and instructions to that effect were given to the respective commanders by their superior. It does not appear, however, that there was uniformly such co-operation.

While the ironclad fleet on April 7, 1863, was attacking the forts and batteries which defended Charleston harbor, General Hunter, commanding the Department of the South, who witnessed that memorable bombardment from the deck of a transport steamer off the bar, on which he had his headquarters, held all of his available force in close proximity, but made no aggressive movement with it.

Admiral DuPont, commanding the South Atlantic squadron, in his reports to the Secretary of the Navy of the ironclad attack and its failure on April 7,

190

admits very frankly that the result had convinced him that Charleston could not be taken by a purely naval attack, and he adds: "The army could give no co-operation."

On May 22 General Hunter wrote a long letter directly to President Lincoln and sent it by the hands of one of his staff officers, reminding the President that six weeks had elapsed since the naval attack on Charleston, an attack of which he says: "From the nature of the Admiral's plans the army could take no active part"; that he had himself been extremely anxious to take advantage of the manifest weakness of the Confederates on Morris Island, to seize that important point, which he was very sure could have been done with great ease; that his troops, which were, he says, "unquestionably the best drilled soldiers in the country," were in readiness and eager to cross Lighthouse Inlet, which was only a few hundred yards wide, and make a descent on Morris Island, and that a foothold secured on that strategic point would make the fall of Fort Sumter as certain as the demonstration of a problem in mathematics. An attempt, however, to seize that island without the co-operation of the navy would be wholly futile and only result in a useless sacrifice of life. He had therefore on the day after the naval attack urged the Admiral to co-operate with him in making that important move. He had sent an officer of his staff to lay his views before Admiral DuPont, but notwithstanding the clearly and elaborately urged advantages of the proposed move the Admiral laconically replied that he "would not fire another shot."

Since then, says General Hunter to the President, he had exercised patience with the Admiral, until he had become "painfully but finally convinced that no aid could be expected from the navy." He feared that Admiral DuPont distrusted the ironclads so much that he was resolved to do nothing with them during the summer. General Hunter therefore urgently begged the President to liberate him from the orders to co-operate with the navy, "which now tie me down to the Admiral's inactivity." And he goes on to develop a plan of operations which he was exceedingly anxious to undertake, if only released from co-operation with the navy, which plan, though interesting, need not be here detailed.

President Lincoln seems to have manifested his disapproval of the proposed plan of campaign, and settled, as he supposed, the question of co-operation between the land and naval forces by relieving both General Hunter and Admiral DuPont from their respective commands.

The selection of a new commander of the Department of the South was indicative of the campaign the Federal Government proposed to make in that department.

General Hunter, in his published report of his own services in the war, says Mr. Lincoln told him that his "temporary suspension" from the command "was due in a great measure to the influence of the Hon. Horace Greeley," who, it seems, as Mr. Lincoln expressed it, "had found the man to do the job" —meaning the capture of Charleston. Moved by this information, General Hunter addressed an angry letter to the distinguished editor, in which he expressed ironically the hope that since Mr. Greeley had taken it upon himself to direct the attack on Charleston, he would be more successful than in his first advance on Richmond, "in which you wasted much ink and other men shed some blood."

But it is not difficult to find other considerations which no doubt had weight in the selection of the new commander. The General-in-Chief of the Army, Halleck, had been an officer of the United States Engineer Corps; so also was his chief of staff, General George W. Cullum. There was naturally and most justly great *esprit de corps* among the officers of that distinguished branch of the military service. The General-in-Chief and his chief of staff, no doubt, believed that an officer of the Engineer Corps was better qualified than an officer of any other arm of the service to direct the operations for the reduction of Charleston, a task requiring military engineering skill of a high order. Under those circumstances, perhaps the following letter from the officer whom Mr. Greeley had found "to do the job" had its weight in the selection of General Hunter's successor, and is given in full as indicative of the plan of campaign to be followed in the Department of the South.

NEW YORK, May 23, 1863.

GENERAL G. W. CULLUM, *Chief of Staff to the General-in-Chief.*

General: It has come to my knowledge that my name has been mentioned to the Secretary of War in connection with the reduction of the forts in Charleston harbor, and it has been urgently suggested to place me in a position where I could direct and control the operations of the land forces against that place. Two or three communications from prominent men here have been sent to the Secretary.

It is not necessary to inform you, who are so well acquainted with me, that I am not in the habit of pushing myself forward or thrusting my professional opinion unasked upon the notice of those in authority. In my daily intercourse with gentlemen of my acquaintance I am, however, always free to answer questions, and I have at sundry times and in sundry places expressed the opinion that the forts in Charleston harbor could be reduced by the means (naval and military combined) now available in the Department of the South, increased by a suitable number of the best heavy rifled guns, provided these have not been sent there since I left the department one year ago.

I have also said that I am willing to risk my own reputation upon an attempt, as I did at Pulaski, provided I could be allowed the untrammeled execution of my own plans (as at Pulaski), except so far as they involve co-operation from the navy.

You are at liberty to show this letter to the General-in-Chief or anyone else.

I expect to remain here until the evening of the 27th instant and then go directly to Cincinnati.

Very respectfully, your obedient servant,

Q. A. GILLMORE, *Brigadier General.*

General Gillmore, of the Volunteers, had served with distinction as a captain of Engineers in the Regular army under Generals Hunter and Benham in the reduction of Fort Pulaski, Georgia, in April, 1862. A few days after the date of the foregoing letter he was ordered to Washington for consultation with the Secretary of War, the General-in-Chief of the Army, and the Assistant Secretary of the

Navy, on the plan of operations for the reduction of Charleston. He seems to have reiterated the opinions already expressed in his letter and to have fully developed his plan of operations.

He urged that there should be cordial and energetic co-operation between the land and naval forces. The part which the latter would be called on to perform in the execution of the proposed plan was represented as one in which "audacity should enter as an important element of success." The commander of the fleet, therefore, should be an officer who had sufficient confidence in the efficiency of the turret ironclads to be "willing to risk his reputation in the development of their new and comparatively untried powers against the harbor defenses of Charleston." Admiral DuPont and his officers commanding the ironclads seem to have been under the impression that the powers of the ironclads had been subjected to very fair and severe test in the attack on the harbor defenses of Charleston on April 7, and the result had not been encouraging.

On June 3 General Gillmore was ordered to relieve General Hunter in command of the Department of the South, and a few days later Admiral Foote, who had distinguished himself in command of gunboats on the Western water, especially in the operations against Fort Donelson, was ordered to relieve Admiral DuPont. Admiral Foote, however, died a few days later, and Admiral Dahlgren was assigned to the command of the South Atlantic squadron.

The Confederate Government still retained General Beauregard in the important command of the Department of South Carolina, Georgia, and Florida, to which he had been assigned in September of the previous year. With the exception of the ironclad attack of April 7 and the concentration of the land forces on that occasion to follow up the expected naval success, no demonstration of moment was made against Charleston from the unsuccessful assault on Secessionville on June 16, 1862, to July 10, 1863. General Beauregard and his predecessor, General Pemberton, had therefore something more than a year in which to complete and enlarge the defensive works which had been planned, and in great measure completed, and to construct others which close examination suggested and the progress of the war had made necessary for the defense of the city.

An important change in the original plan of defense had been made by General Pemberton, in the abandonment of Cole's Island at the southwestern extremity of James Island, an important strategic point of the outer defenses commanding the entrance to the Stono River. General Beauregard regarded the abandonment of Cole's Island as a fatal mistake; so did General Ripley, to whom, perhaps, more than to any other officer, Charleston was indebted for the system of defensive works which, together with the works which had been constructed before the war, enabled a comparatively small force to hold the enemy at bay and keep them away from the city during the war. The abandonment of Cole's Island had made necessary the construction of a long line of works for the defense of James Island, which was justly regarded as the key by land to Charleston.

More than a year had elapsed during which, with the exception of April 7, the active war which was devastating other parts of the country had not come nigh Charleston. The time had now arrived, and was to continue for about twenty months, when the thunder of artillery—the sound, which no words can describe, of the heavy rifle shots as they flew through the air, day and night, bursting over and in their city and crashing through their houses—was to become as familiar to her inhabitants as are the noises of passing vehicles over the streets to the dwellers in more fortunate cities. History may perhaps record the military skill, steadfast fidelity, and gallantry with which the city was defended, but the heroic fortitude, cheerful courage, and patient endurance with which her non-combatant population bore the hardships of the siege and the adversity of the more trying period which followed it will probably never be fully told.

It is as difficult to follow understandingly a narrative of military operations without the aid of a good map as it is to comprehend the demonstration of a complicated proposition in geometry without the aid of a diagram. No description of the country will adequately supply the place of a good map. A brief description, however, of the limited scene of the impending operations may aid those not familiar with the locality to a better understanding of them.

The city of Charleston is at the extremity of the narrow peninsula between the Cooper and Ashley rivers. James Island, to the south and east, is separated from the city by Ashley River, and from St. John's Island, to the south and west, by the Stono River. In greatest extent from north to south it is about 9 miles and from east to west about 7 miles. On its sea front it is bordered by a narrow sandbank extending from the entrance to Charleston harbor to Stono Inlet, about 11 miles in length. About 3¾ miles from the northern extremity this bank has been cut through by the waters of the ocean, thus dividing it into two islands. The northern part is Morris Island, the southern Folly Island. The channel between them is called Lighthouse Inlet. These islands are separated from the firm land of James Island by Folly River and Creek, Vincent's Creek, and impassable marshes which are subject to overflow by very high tides and are intersected by numerous, tortuous, narrow, but deep, streams.

The northern extremity of Morris Island, which is called Cumming's Point, and Sullivan's Island to the northeast, border the entrance to Charleston harbor. Fort Moultrie is near the western end of Sullivan's Island and distant 2700 yards from Cumming's Point, on which the Confederates had constructed a work called Battery Gregg. Fort Sumter was a brick work of three tiers of guns, built on an artificial island or foundation south of the channel, nearly midway between Sullivan's and James' islands, about 1760 yards from Fort Moultrie on the former,

1980 yards from Fort Johnson on the latter, 1390 yards from Cumming's Point and 3½ miles from the city of Charleston.

About 1300 yards from Cumming's Point, at a very narrow part of Morris Island, was an earthwork of considerable development and strength called Battery Wagner, which extended from the beach on the east to Vincent Creek on the west, presenting to the southwest a front of about 275 yards.

The island is wider in its southern than in its northern part, the southern extremity on Lighthouse Inlet being about 1000 yards in width. Its surface is irregular and broken by sand ridges, forming at many points secure shelter for troops. It has an area of about 400 acres, its middle point is 5⅜ of a mile from the nearest point of Charleston, and the main channel into the harbor is parallel to and at about an average distance of 1200 yards from it.

This small sand island has been thus minutely and tediously described because it was destined to be the camp home for nearly two years of many thousands of men; it was to become famous as the scene of a siege which will be memorable in military history and one of the most formidable bombardments of which there is any record, the scene of great labor and exposure, much desperate fighting, of sickness and death in all the frightful forms incident to war and to wasting fevers.

General Gillmore assumed command of the department on June 12, 1863, with his headquarters at Hilton Head. His troops held the coast from Lighthouse Inlet to St. Augustine, a distance of about 250 miles, but the great mass of the force was in South Carolina and near Charleston. He had ample steamboat transportation at his command and could readily and rapidly concentrate his forces whenever and wherever on the coast he desired to have them. He entered on the duty assigned him untrammeled by instructions, free to carry out his own plans, assured of the liberal support of his government in supplying him with all requisite material for the successful accomplishment of the plan he had proposed, and which had been approved after full and free discussion by a mixed board of officers of the army and navy.

Of the several plans of operation against Charleston which naturally suggest themselves, that by way of James Island, which it was generally believed offered the surest and speediest avenue to success, had been attempted and abandoned after the unsuccessful assault on Secessionville in June, 1862. So, too, the plan of a forcible entrance of the fleet into the harbor had been attempted and failed on April 7.

Of all the plans that by way of Morris Island was regarded as the easiest of accomplishment in its first steps. The land force was already in possession of Folly Island. To cross over the narrow channel of Lighthouse Inlet and secure a foothold on Morris Island with the aid of the navy would be very easily accomplished, and in the succeeding operations on that island the navy could render ready and efficient aid, having always close at hand in North Edisto Inlet a secure harbor of refuge in the

event of stormy weather; an important consideration, because the monitors were not suitable to ride
in safety in stormy waters.

But possession of Morris Island would be very
far from decisive of the fate of Charleston. Secure
possession of James Island, the forces remaining
relatively the same, would, it was believed, lead
inevitably to the reduction of Charleston, whereas
possession of Morris Island would be only a means
to the probable but remote accomplishment of the
same end.

Fort Sumter was regarded as the chief obstacle in
the way of the navy in any attempt which it might
make to enter the harbor. If that fort could be reduced, or its defensive power destroyed, the fleet, it
was argued, could readily remove the obstructions,
force an entrance into the harbor, and compel the
surrender of the city, when the evacuation of the
harbor defenses would necessarily follow. It was
admitted that the navy alone could not capture
Sumter, or even so cripple it as to render it harm-
less. That must be done by the combined land and
naval forces, and General Gillmore had been selected
to command the Department of the South and Admiral Dahlgren the South Atlantic squadron, for the
express purpose of carrying into execution the plan
of operations which the former had proposed for
the reduction of Fort Sumter and then the capture
of Charleston.

General Gillmore's plan of operations briefly
stated was:

First. Make a descent upon and take possession of the south end of Morris Island.

Second. To lay siege to and reduce Battery Wagner, a strong earthwork near the north end of the island and about twenty-six hundred yards from Fort Sumter. The reduction of Battery Wagner would necessitate the fall of Battery Gregg on Cumming's Point.

Third. From the positions thus secured to demolish Fort Sumter and co-operate with the navy in a heavy artillery fire when it should be ready to move forward.

Fourth. The ironclad fleet to remove the channel obstructions, run by the batteries on Sullivan's and James islands, reach the city and compel its surrender.

The army was to take the lead in all but the fourth of these distinct operations. Admiral Dahlgren says there had been no understanding between him and General Gillmore as to the fourth of these distinct operations.

When General Gillmore assumed command of the department preparations for entering on the execution of his plan of operations were already well advanced. Early in the preceding April General Vogdes had been assigned to the command of the troops on Folly Island. His aggregate force for the three months of April, May, and June varied from about 4700 to 6000, or an average of about 5350. It was actively employed in preparing the island as a land base of operations against Charleston, for which it possessed many advantages.

The woods and dense undergrowth, chiefly of palmetto, together with the sand hills, screened the General's operations from view and shielded his troops from fire. It had, besides this, further advantage in that it served as a base of operations either by way of James or Morris Island. By the 3d of July, under the immediate direction of the accomplished officers, Lieutenants Suter and Michie, of the United States Engineers, not only had the necessary defensive batteries been constructed for the security of the islands, but others for the special purpose of covering the descent on Morris Island. These last mentioned batteries were constructed on the northern end of the island called Little Folly Island. The thick growth and sand hills of that locality thoroughly screened the workmen from view.

The movements of troops were made and the labor performed mainly in the night and every precaution was taken to conceal the operations from the Confederates. So important was secrecy in the matter regarded, that a blockade-runner, the *Dart*, which to escape pursuit had been run ashore a little south of Lighthouse Inlet, was permitted to be wrecked by the Confederates and the cargo carried off, when it could easily have been prevented by guns already in position. The troops did not even return the brisk Confederate fire which was kept on that end of the island while the wrecking of the *Dart* was in progress, though several men who were at work on the batteries were killed and wounded.

In this way batteries were carefully constructed, renetted, and embrasured, magazines and splinter-proofs made, thirty-two rifled guns, varying from 10- to 30-pounders, twelve 10-inch and four 8-inch mortars were mounted, and under the energetic management of the ordnance officer, Captain Mordecai, each gun was supplied with two hundred rounds of ammunition. All this was done within from six hundred to eight hundred yards of the Confederate pickets on the south end of Morris Island.

General Vogdes claims, as does General Gillmore, that the existence of the batteries was not known to the Confederates until they were unmasked and had opened fire. General Beauregard says "the attack was not a surprise, neither was the erection of the enemy's works on Little Folly Island unknown to the local commanders or these headquarters." That the enemy was in large force and very busily at work on the island was unquestionably known to the local commanders, and to General Beauregard, but they could scarcely have known the positions and extent of the works constructed against them. General Ripley, in whose district Morris Island was, says in his official report to General Beauregard: "On the morning of the 10th the enemy opened a heavy fire upon our positions from Little Folly with from twenty to thirty long-range guns, which he had placed in position during the night," whereas the fire had been from forty-seven guns in batteries, which had been in course of construction nearly a month, and had been ready for action a week before they were unmasked and opened.

On the other side of Lighthouse Inlet, on the south end of Morris Island, the Confederates had partially constructed eight one-gun batteries and two mortar batteries, one for two, the other for one mortar. All were detached and stretched along the sand ridge, designed to protect the beach, and they were very incomplete. Rifle-pits or infantry epaulments were also made, extending westward toward Oyster Point.

While General Beauregard knew perfectly well that Folly Island was occupied in large force and was in course of preparation for both defensive and offensive operations, and was confident that a blow from it was impending, he could not know with certainty where it would be directed. Regarding James Island as unquestionably the vital point in the land defenses of Charleston, and not having sufficient force, labor, and heavy guns for the thorough defense of both James and Morris islands, he had employed his inadequate force and means chiefly in putting the former (James Island) in a secure defensive state. Hence the comparatively defenseless state of the south end of Morris Island.

On July 6 Admiral Dahlgren assumed command of the South Atlantic squadron at Port Royal. A day or two later, after a conference between the commanders of the land and naval forces, General Gillmore transferred his headquarters from Hilton Head to Folly Island, and about the same time Brigadier General Truman Seymour was assigned to the command of a division embracing the troops serving on that island.

On entering upon the execution of his plan of operations, General Gillmore assumed erroneously that his adversary greatly outnumbered him. His tri-monthly report for July 10 shows his aggregate force present in the department, exclusive of the sick, to have been 20,837. In his official report he states his effective force to have been at that time 17,463. He was untrammeled with instructions, and it was therefore left to his own discretion to employ such part of his force as he thought proper in the execution of the plans on which he was about to enter.

At that time General Beauregard's force had been reduced by detachments sent to other armies. The battle of Gettysburg had been fought and lost by the Confederates, and General Lee was calmly and defiantly confronting his victorious enemy, with his back to the flooded Potomac, waiting for it to fall sufficiently for him to cross and continue his march into Virginia; Vicksburg and Port Hudson had fallen, and General Rosecrans, by skillful maneuvering, had pressed General Bragg's army across the Tennessee. General Beauregard therefore, like other department commanders, had been called on to detach troops and send them to Virginia and the West. On July 10 the "grand total" of his force of all arms in South Carolina and Georgia was 15,318, being 28,000 less than he had estimated as necessary when he assumed command.

Of that force 5841 were in the First Military Division, which embraced James, Morris, and Sullivan's islands and the city of Charleston, Brigadier

General Ripley commanding. There were but 2906 men on James Island and 927 on Morris Island, including the garrisons of Batteries Wagner and Gregg.[1]

No plan of operations by land against Charleston seems to have been regarded as complete which did not embrace an expedition to cut the Charleston & Savannah Railroad. On this occasion the execution of that part of the plan was entrusted to Colonel Higginson, who on the 9th started from Beaufort with a regiment in two armed steamboats, accompanied by a small gunboat, the object being to go up the Edisto River to Jacksborough, and destroy the railroad bridge and as much of the road as practicable. Under cover of a dense fog the party reached Willstown Bluff unperceived and moved up toward the village.

The line of railroad had been nearly stripped of troops for the defense of Charleston. A section of the Chestnut field artillery, Lieutenant T. G. White, and a few cavalrymen, under Colonel Aiken, near Willstown, not being in condition to offer effective resistance, fell back after some skirmishing. The Federal troops delayed there long enough to plunder the place, burn Mr. Morris' mill and barns, and carry off about one hundred and thirty negroes, chiefly women and children.

The expedition then proceeded up the river, but

[1]General Beauregard's report shows that on July 10 he had in South Carolina 3461 infantry, 3664 artillery, and 2651 cavalry. Total, 9776. In Georgia, 1745 infantry, 2130 artillery, and 1667 cavalry. Total, 5542.

the delay at Willstown had given time for a section of the Washington Artillery, of Charleston, Lieutenant I. R. Horsey commanding, supported by a platoon of cavalry, under Lieutenant John Banskett, to reach the river; when the steamers were within three miles of Jacksborough, opposite Dr. Glover's plantation, the field guns opened upon them; the boats stopped, hesitated, and turned back, followed by the section of the Washington Artillery and also a section of the Marion Artillery, Lieutenant Robert Murdoch commanding, which kept up the fire until one steamer was so crippled as to become unmanageable and ran aground, when it was set on fire and burned. The other two steamed out of range and returned to Beaufort.

The two field guns of the steamer were taken uninjured from the burned vessel and were soon in Confederate service. General Gillmore in his official report dismisses this expedition with the brief remark: "It signally failed, with a loss to us of two pieces of field artillery and a small steamer, which was burned to prevent its falling into the hands of the enemy."

Colonel H. K. Aiken, commanding the Confederates, claims that it was burned by the fire of the Confederate field guns of the Macon Artillery. But for the delay at Willstown Colonel Higginson might have destroyed the bridge and damaged the road, or at least have retarded the reinforcements which soon passed over from Savannah.

To draw attention, and perhaps troops, from Morris to James Island and produce the impression that the latter was to be the point of attack, General Gillmore sent General A. H. Terry, with 3800 men in armed transports, up the Stono, conveyed by the gunboats *Pawnee, Marblehead,* and *McDonough,* Captain Balch commanding. Under cover of the naval guns from the steamers in the Stono and Little Folly rivers, which thoroughly swept the ground in front, the troops landed on Battery Island and Grimble's place, moved forward in a threatening manner and brisk skirmishing commenced between the pickets. General Terry's force outnumbered by several hundred men all the infantry General Beauregard had in South Carolina and by more than a thousand all the infantry and artillery combined on James Island.

General Gillmore believed that his feint on James Island had produced at least one of the effects desired, in drawing troops from Morris Island; but he was mistaken. In truth, there were no troops that could have been drawn from that island without abandoning at least the south end and leaving the whole island in great jeopardy.

It had been General Gillmore's intention to make the descent on Morris Island about midnight between the 8th and 9th. He had given detailed instructions to that effect, which were so far carried out that obstructions in Little Folly Creek were removed by a party of the First New York Engineer Regiment and the batteries were so far unmasked as to disclose their presence to the Confederates. That same night Captain Charles T. Haskell, of the First South Carolina Infantry, visited Little Folly Island with a scouting party, and discovered the company's barges or launches collected in the creeks approaching the inlet. During the whole of the 9th, therefore, there were abundant indications that an attack was immediately impending.

General George C. Strong was selected to lead in the attack with his brigade. He was a young officer of the Ordnance Corps, who had graduated with high honors at West Point in the class of 1858 and had distinguished himself in the war both in Virginia and Louisiana. His brigade was composed of the Sixth Connecticut Regiment, Colonel John L. Chatfield; Forty-eighth New York, Colonel Barton; Third New Hampshire, Colonel Jackson; Ninth Maine, Colonel Emory; Seventy-sixth Pennsylvania, Colonel Strawbridge; battalion of four companies Seventh Connecticut, Lieutenant Colonel Rodman; Company C, Third Rhode Island Artillery; detachment Third United States Artillery; detachment First New York Engineers.

A battalion of the Forty-eighth New York, the colonel commanding, and the detachments of artillery were left on the island with General Vogdes.

The brigade was embarked on launches near the south end of Folly Island early in the night of the 9th, and, conveyed four naval howitzer launches, Lieutenant Bunce commanding, moved up Folly River and Creek and halted near the entrance to Lighthouse Inlet, where they were screened from view by tall marsh grass, and there awaited the signal to advance.

The remaining force on Folly Island was held in reserve under General Vogdes. The Sixty-second Ohio, Colonel Pond; Sixty-seventh Ohio, Colonel Voorhees, and Eighty-fifth Pennsylvania, Colonel Howell, were near the signal station. The Seventh New Hampshire, Colonel H. S. Putnam; One Hundredth New York, Colonel Dandy; a battalion of six companies of the Forty-eighth New York, Colonel Barker, and Battery B, First United States Artillery, Captain G. V. Henry commanding, were at the northern end of Little Folly Island, in readiness to follow General Strong's Brigade. The formidable batteries which were to perform so important a part were commanded by Lieutenant Colonel Jackson and Major L. L. Langton, First United States Artillery.

Just across Lighthouse Inlet and within easy range were the detached Confederate battery of eight guns and three mortars, manned by two companies of the First South Carolina Artillery, Captains J. C. Mitchell and J. R. Macbeth commanding, supported by the Twenty-first South Carolina Infantry, about four hundred men, Major McIver commanding, and a detachment of the First South Carolina Infantry, under Captain Charles T. Haskell (in all about seven hundred). The garrison of Battery Wagner, about three miles distant on the island, was two companies of artillery, Captains C. E. Chichester and J. R. Mathews commanding, and of Battery Gregg, Captain Henry R. Lesesne's company of artillery. All of the artillery on the island was commanded by Lieutenant Colonel J. A. Yates, First South Carolina Artillery. The whole force was commanded by Colonel R. F. Graham, Twenty-first South Carolina Infantry.

As the sun rose on the morning of July 10 the Federal batteries were unmasked and thirty-two guns and fifteen mortars opened fire, to which the Confederates promptly replied. A few minutes later four monitors, the *Weehawken*, Commander E. R. Calhoun, the *Nahant*, Commander John Downs, the *Kaatskill*, Commander George H. Rodgers, and the *Montauk*, Commander D. McN. Fairfax, which had crossed the bar and taken positions from which some of the Confederate batteries could be enfiladed and others taken in reverse, opened fire with fifteen- and eleven-inch guns on the Confederate left; the four howitzer launches pulled into position and opened on the right, and for nearly three hours about sixty guns, some of them of the heaviest caliber, concentrated a rapid and accurate fire on the Confederate position, to which the Confederates as rapidly replied.

A little after seven o'clock the signal was given to General Strong to cross the inlet, land, and assail the batteries, and he pulled with the greater part of his brigade directly and rapidly for Oyster Point, the extreme left of the Confederate position. As soon as the launches came into view some of the Confederate guns were turned on them with effect, destroying one of them, while the infantry hastened to the Point to dispute the landing.

Colonel Chatfield, with his regiment, the Sixth Connecticut, had pulled rapidly to the right, or southeastern, extremity of the island, and the tide being low the bank sheltered him from the fire of the guns on the sand hills, which were about thirty feet high—so high that the guns could not be trained on the boats.

Both parties landed successfully and with little loss. The battalion of four companies of the Seventh Connecticut, Lieutenant Colonel Rodman, was the first to land at Oyster Point, quickly followed by the battalions of the Forty-eighth New York, Ninth Maine, Third New Hampshire, and Seventy-sixth Pennsylvania.

The launches immediately crossed to Little Folly Island, and in twenty minutes from the time they touched the beach the Seventh New Hampshire, One Hundredth New York, the battalion of the Forty-eighth New York, and Captain Henry's battery of the First Artillery were transported to and landed on the south end of Morris Island.

In the meantime the main column at Oyster Point had formed in line and advanced against the Twenty-first South Carolina, while Colonel Chatfield advanced directly against the batteries, throwing out strong skirmishing parties on the right and left, which soon flanked the batteries, taking them in reverse. After an obstinate resistance, what was left of the artillery had to abandon their guns and retire. In truth, the batteries had been for nearly three hours enveloped in fire and overwhelmed by the weight of metal thrown on them.

Colonel Graham, finding his little band of infantry, which had lost heavily, in danger of being cut off by Colonel Chatfield's column and captured by General Strong's, ordered it to fall back to Battery Wagner.

The two Federal columns, converging upon the batteries, captured them all, one after the other, and pursued the retreating Confederates, while the monitors, steaming slowly parallel to the beach, continued their fire upon the shattered Confederates.

The Seventh Battalion South Carolina Infantry, Lieutenant Colonel Nelson, had been ordered to reinforce Morris Island, but did not arrive in time to take part in the battle. Two companies of it, which arrived first, had been ordered forward to support the batteries, but met the retreating Confederates and were warmly engaged in endeavoring to cover the retreat.

The Federals continued the pursuit until they came within range of the guns of Battery Wagner, which opened rapidly and the pursuit ceased.

The weather was excessively hot, so, too, was the fire from Wagner, say the Federal reports, "riddling" the colors of the Sixth Connecticut. The men were too much exhausted to storm Battery Wagner. They were therefore halted a few hundred yards from it, where the sand hills sheltered them from its fire, and threw up breastworks for better protection.

The monitors took position abreast of Wagner and kept up a brisk fire on it for the remainder of the day, except (and this appears to have been a custom in the navy which seems strange to soldiers) that "at noon we hauled out of fire to give the men dinner and about two o'clock went back and resumed work," says the Admiral. Wagner returned the fire with spirit from a ten-inch columbiad, her only effective gun against the monitors. The *Kaatskill*, against which the fire was mainly directed, was struck sixty times, her deck crashed through and pierced in several places, letting in water very freely.

By nine o'clock in the morning the affair on land was over and two-thirds of Morris Island was in possession of the Federal troops. The descent had been made with complete success and little loss (General Strong reports fifteen killed and ninety-two wounded). Among the killed was Captain Lent, of the Forty-eighth New York. They had captured three 8-inch navy shell guns, two 8-inch seacoast howitzers, one rifled 24-pounder, one 30-pounder, one 12-pounder Whitworth and three 10-inch seacoast mortars—in all eleven pieces—the camp equipage, and 127 prisoners.

The little band of Confederates had made a gallant stand for three hours against great odds, and had not retreated until it was absolutely necessary to escape capture and until, out of a total force not exceeding 700, they had lost 294 killed, wounded, and missing, "among whom," says General Ripley, "I mention with especial regret the following officers: Captains John R. Chevers and Haskell and Lieutenant J. S. Bee, who had rendered important service previous to and behaved with distinguished gallantry in the engagement."

General Seymour commended very highly the conduct of his troops on the occasion:

"For the brilliant vigor," he says, "with which the movements of his brigade were conducted the greatest credit is due to Brigadier General Strong, whose personal example was heroism itself. His report justly praises his subordinate commanders, and to those I must refer, but I must mention particularly the excellent conduct of Colonel Chatfield, Sixth Connecticut, who led his regiment in the advance up Morris Island until its colors were riddled by the close fire from Battery Wagner. But to the hearty devotion and the cheerful courage of the soldiers of this division, in the patient labors in preparing for the battle and the ready courage with which they fought it, must, after all, be given the highest honors, and their gallant conduct in this brilliant action will always be to their commanders and their country the source of just pride."

The assault of Battery Wagner, which the troops were too much exhausted to attempt on the 10th, was made about day dawn the next morning by General Strong.

The garrison of Wagner at that time consisted of the shattered remainder of the troops which had contested the landing the previous morning, namely, the Twenty-first South Carolina Regiment, about two hundred men, under Major J. G. W. McIver; twenty men of Company D, First South Carolina Infantry, Lieutenant Horlbeck commanding, and seventy men of Companies E, H, and I, First South Carolina Artillery, under Captain John C. Mitchell; also the Gist Guard, Captain C. E. Chichester; Mathews' Artillery, Captain J. R. Mathews, which

had occupied the battery on the 10th; the Seventh
South Carolina Battalion, about three hundred men,
Major J. H. Rion commanding; four companies
each of the First Georgia Regiment, Colonel C. H.
Olmstead; the Twelfth Georgia Battalion, Lieu-
tenant Colonel H. D. Capers, and three companies
of the Eighteenth Georgia Battalion, Major W. S.
Basinger; in all about five hundred men, Colonel
Olmstead commanding. The aggregate force was
about twelve hundred men.

The South Carolinians manned the guns and the
right and right center of the ramparts. The
Georgians, who arrived in the night of the 10th,
guarded the left and left center of the work. The
Eighteenth Battalion occupied the southeast bastion,
the First Georgia along the sea front to the left, the
Twelfth Georgia Battalion to the right, connecting
with the Carolinians. Lieutenant Colonel Yates
commanded the artillery and Colonel R. F. Graham
(Twenty-first South Carolina) the whole.

General Strong formed his brigade before day-
dawn. The assaulting column consisted of the battalion of the Seventh Connecticut, the Seventy-sixth
Pennsylvania, and the Ninth Maine. As on the
previous morning, the Seventh Connecticut led the
advance, Lieutenant Colonel Rodman commanding.
The Third and Seventh New Hampshire were held
in reserve. The battalion of the Seventh Connecticut was deployed in line in front, followed
closely in the order named by the Seventy-sixth
Pennsylvania and Ninth Maine, each formed in
close divisions. They were ordered to carefully

preserve their intervals and when the Confederates should open fire to rush forward with a cheer, mount the parapet and carry the battery by storm.

General Strong commanded in person. His instructions were most faithfully carried out by Lieutenant Colonel Rodman, who led his Seventh Connecticut men under a brisk fire of cannon and musketry to the ditch and some of them to the top of the parapet, where, it is reported, they bayoneted two Confederate gunners.

"But unfortunately," says General Strong in his report, "when the enemy opened fire simultaneously along the whole line, and with a range of two hundred yards, the Seventy-sixth Pennsylvania halted and lay down upon the ground. Though they remained in this position but a few moments and afterwards moved gallantly forward, some of them even to the ditch, that halt lost the battle, for the interval was lost and the Seventh Connecticut, unsupported, were driven from the parapet. The whole column, including the Ninth Maine, which had reached the ditch on the left, gave way and retreated from the field."

The garrison of Wagner had of course expected an attack and was on the alert all night. When the column was seen advancing in the dim light of early dawn Colonel Graham deliberately held his fire until his enemy was within close range, then opened simultaneously along his whole line, firing rapidly and continuously until the last man of the fast retreating column was under cover of the sand hills.

The Seventh Connecticut was particularly distinguished on this occasion. Unsupported and when there seemed no hope of success, some of the men persisted with great daring in their efforts to force an entrance into the work. One brave man sprang to the parapet in front of a thirty-two-pounder, double-charged with grape shot. Lieutenant Gilchrist, of South Carolina, in command of the gun, struck by the man's fearless bearing, called to him to come in before the gun was fired. As quick as thought the man's rifle was leveled and a ball whizzed by Gilchrist's head. The discharge of the gun followed and the man was hurled across the ditch a mangled corpse. This regiment had been the first to enter Fort Pulaski when it was captured the year before and the officers and men had behaved with much kindness toward Colonel Olmstead and his men who were captured on that occasion. Among the prisoners captured at this time were many of this regiment, who recognized their former prisoners, calling them by name, and were received by them with as much kind consideration as the circumstances permitted.

General Strong in his official report to General Gillmore, made on the day of the assault, states that his loss that morning was 8 officers and 322 non-commissioned officers and privates. Among the severely wounded was Lieutenant Colonel Rodman of the Seventh Connecticut. Captain Gray, who succeeded to the command of the battalion of the Seventh Connecticut, reports that 191 men of the battalion went to the assault and that 103 of them were killed, wounded, and missing, and he adds that their mess contained 11 officers that morning before the assault and but 4 after it.

The Confederate loss in the assault was 1 officer and 5 enlisted men killed and 1 officer and 5 enlisted men wounded. Captain Werner, First Georgia, and Edward Postelle, of the Eighteenth Georgia, were killed, Lieutenant Frederick Tupper, Eighteenth Georgia Battalion, severely wounded. Colonel Graham reports that he captured 130 and buried over 100 of the Federal troops.

The Federal losses on the mornings of the 10th and 11th, as officially reported by General Strong, who commanded in person on both occasions, aggregated 436. In an official letter from General Gillmore to General Halleck reporting the success of his descent on Morris Island, he says, speaking of the assault on the morning of the 11th: "The parapet was gained, but the support recoiled under the fire to which they were exposed and could not be got up. Our loss in both actions (the mornings of the 10th and 11th) will not vary much from 150."

A more substantial and obvious reason for the failure of the assault will naturally suggest itself to the most causal reader than that assigned by General Strong, namely, the brief halt of the Seventy-sixth Pennsylvania. The probable cause of the failure was that the assaulting column was too weak numerically. It scarcely outnumbered the garrison, which had all the advantages of position within a strong field work.

There seems to have been some difference of

opinion between Generals Gillmore and Seymour as to this point—on which of them did the responsibility of the assault, as it was made, rest.   The former commanded the department, the latter a division of the troops on the island, and the assault was made by a part only of one of his brigades.   General Gillmore, in an elaborate report of his operations, makes but brief mention of the assault, saying merely: "General Seymour was ordered to carry Fort Wagner by assault by daybreak on the following morning.   The attempt failed."

General Seymour says: "Before daylight on the 11th an assault had been made by Brigadier General Strong, with his brigade, in accordance with instructions given to him directly by Brigadier General Gillmore, which attack failed from the complete preparation of the enemy, due to his pickets having been driven in an hour before the attempted surprise." General Strong reports officially that the assault was made "pursuant to instructions from department headquarters."

Immediately after the assault, in a conference between General Gillmore and Admiral Dahlgren, it was decided that the parapets of Wagner should be battered down and its guns silenced by a combined fire from land and naval batteries before making the next assault.

CHAPTER XI.

The failure of the Federal assault on Battery Wagner on the morning of July 11, 1863, convinced General Gillmore that before making another attempt to carry that work by storm it would be expedient, at least, if not absolutely necessary, to silence its guns and cut down its parapets, scarp and counterscarp, by a combined and heavy artillery fire from the land and naval batteries.

Admiral Dahlgren concurred in this opinion and was quite ready to perform his part of the bombardment. The naval batteries were ready and could be placed in and taken out of position at pleasure. The mortar vessels, at a secure distance beyond the range of the Confederate guns, having ascertained the range, could drop their shells into Battery Wagner without danger from the return fire, while the monitors, with their batteries securely encased within iron plating of eleven inches thickness, could steam into position and maintain their fire as long as it suited the Admiral, steaming out of range again with great regularity at stated intervals, that the men might take their meals and accustomed rest undisturbed by the Confederate guns, and return to their work with the regularity of gangs of laborers engaged in other and more productive industry.

But it was not so with the land batteries. It was necessary to construct and arm them under the fires of several Confederate batteries on Morris and James islands and Fort Sumter. The daily fire of the ironclads generally suppressed in a great measure the fire of Wagner while the land forces were contructing their batteries. But this daily firing of the ironclads was not always made with impunity. Though there was but one gun in Wagner that could reach them with much effect,—a 10-inch columbiad,—that one gun under the cool and skillful management of Captain Frazer Matthews was fired with accuracy, doing much damage to the monitors, one of which was seen on the evening of the 12th going southward without a smokestack and apparently much crippled. But in spite of the Confederate fire the work on the land batteries was pressed forward rapidly night and day and completed in the course of a week.

In the meantime the Confederates were making every possible exertion to strengthen and increase the armament of works already constructed, and to construct others which the Federal operations on Morris Island and the safety of Charleston suggested as necessary. The armament of Wagner was increased by four 12-pounder howitzers and two 32-pounder carronades. In response to General Beauregard's earnest call for reinforcements, General Clingman had been sent to him with his brigade from North Carolina, and General A. H. Colquitt had arrived with two regiments of his Georgia brigade. The Eleventh South Carolina Regiment and Marion Light Artillery had been brought to Charleston from the line of the Charleston & Savannah Railroad, but the importance of guarding that road very soon made it necessary to return them to that duty.

The arrival of these reinforcements naturally suggested the question whether or not it was practicable to drive the Federal force from Morris Island. In a consultation with his general officers, Ripley, Taliaferro, Hagood, and Jordan (chief of staff), and Colonel E. B. Harris, chief of engineers, General Beauregard presented that question for consideration. The number of troops deemed necessary to attack the enemy on Morris Island with reasonable prospect of success was estimated at four thousand, the area and the general shape of the island making it impracticable to employ a larger force to advantage. To carry out this plan it would be necessary to throw the four thousand troops on the island during the night and attack and defeat the enemy before daylight. To make the movement and attack in daylight would expose the Confederates to the flank fire of the naval guns. Seeing that the Federal force was about seven thousand, covered by defensive works, to attack it in front and in the light of day, with the ironclads pouring in a destructive fire on the flank, could scarcely be hoped to prove successful. With the very insufficient means of transportation at General Beauregard's command, it was deemed impracticable to throw a sufficient force on the island, move upon the enemy, and make the attack during a single night. The idea was therefore abandoned and a purely defensive plan of operations was then determined on.

The presence of General Terry at Legare's and Grimble's, on James Island, with a larger force than the Confederates had on the same island was a standing menace to the latter, which it was important to suppress. General Johnson Hagood commanded the Confederates on that island, and General Colquitt, having arrived on the 14th with two regiments o his Georgia brigade, was sent to reinforce him. Early on the morning of the 16th a reconnoissance in force was made on the enemy, Generals Hagood and Colquitt commanding in person. The enemy occupied Battery Island and parts of Legare's and Grimble's plantations. The naval gunboats were in the Stono and other armed steamers were in Folly River, giving a cross fire which could sweep the ground in front as far as the Confederate pickets. The object of the movement was limited to driving in the pickets on the left, making a reconnoissance of that part of their position, capturing or destroying the part of the force nearest Grimble's, and driving off and, if possible, crippling the gunboats *Pawnee* and *Marblehead,* which were anchored highest up the Stono.

General Colquitt, with the Twenty-fifth South

Carolina, Lieutenant Colonel J. G. Presley commanding; Sixth Georgia, Colonel J. T. Lofton commanding; Nineteenth Georgia, Colonel A. J. Hutchins; four companies of the Thirty-second Georgia, Lieutenant Colonel W. H. Pruden commanding, and Captain E. L. Parker's Battery of Artillery, in all about fourteen hundred men, were ordered to cross the marsh dividing Legare's from Grimble's plantation at the crossing nearest Secessionville, driving the enemy as far as the lower crossing near the Stono, recross the marsh by a flank movement and cut off and capture the force at Grimble's. Colonel C. H. Way, of the Fifty-fourth Georgia, with about eight hundred infantry of his own and the Thirty-first North Carolina Regiment, followed in echelon on the Grimble side of the marsh to co-operate with Colquitt. A reserve of a section of artillery, supported by a company of infantry and a squadron of cavalry, under Lieutenant Colonel R. J. Jeffords, Fifth South Carolina Cavalry, was held in hand near Rivers' house. On the right Lieutenant Colonel Del. Kemper, with four rifled 12-pounders and four Napoleon guns, supported by Colonel James D. Radcliffe, of the Sixty-first North Carolina, with about four hundred men of his own regiment, was ordered to attack the gunboats in the Stono.

The movement was made at day dawn. Six companies of the Twenty-fifth South Carolina deployed as skirmishers on the right and left of the road leading from Secessionville to Legare's house, pressed forward, rapidly crossed Rivers' causeway,

where the Federal picket line (Fifty-fourth Massachusetts) was encountered and driven back hastily
on the main line, which retired to Battery Island,
"leaving their camp strewn with muskets, accouter-
ments, blankets, overcoats, prisoners," etc., says
Colonel Way. As soon as the picket firing commenced the party at Grimble's, which was smaller
than had been supposed, fled to Battery Island and so
escaped capture. There was some brisk firing of
field guns on both sides. A company of the Nineteenth Georgia pursued a party of the Fifty-fourth
Massachusetts, which had been cut off by the left of
the advancing skirmish line, killing and wounding a
number of them, the others escaping through the
marsh.

Colonel Radcliffe and Lieutenant Colonel Kemper surprised the *Pawnee*, (Captain Balch commanding), and *Marblehead* at early dawn by a
rapid and accurate fire, striking the *Pawnee* forty-
two times with considerable effect. From the nature of their position in the Stono the gunboats could
not bring their guns to bear with effect on the troops,
but fell down the river out of range of the field
guns and in positions where their own batteries
could be used, and in response to a signal from
General Terry the gunboats swept the ground in the
Federal front, rendering valuable service, for which
General Terry was quick to acknowledge his in-
debtedness to the naval commander.

The object of the reconnoissance having been accomplished, the Confederates retired, and that night
General Terry abandoned the island, carrying his

force to Folly Island, and the Confederates occupied the positions from which the Federals had retired. The loss in the affair had been slight—about fifty on the Federal and eighteen on the Confederate side. The desired result was accomplished when the Federal force withdrew from the island.

Service in Battery Wagner was necessarily one of ceaseless vigilance, entailing on officers and men such continued mental and physical strain that it was necessary to relieve the garrison by fresh troops at short intervals. It was General Beauregard's wish that it should be relieved every forty-eight hours, but the change had to be made in boats during the night and soon became so difficult that the tour of duty was extended. Brigadier General William B. Taliaferro, who was on duty at Savannah when the descent was made on Morris Island, hastened to Charleston on leave of absence for a few hours and solicited service in the defense of the city. His offer was accepted and he was assigned to the command of Battery Wagner on the 13th.

To guard against surprise a line of rifle-pits was made across the island, about two hundred yards in front of the work. The Federal advance picket line was about three-quarters of a mile distant and could be seen from the parapet of Wagner. Beyond that point the enemy was concealed by sand hills and neither their numbers nor the extent of the preparations they were making were known.

To gain information on those points, cover the men who were digging the rifle-pits, and inspirit the garrison by an aggressive movement, General Taliaferro ordered a sortie to be made on the night of the 14th, with one hundred and fifty men detailed from the infantry of the garrison, namely, the Fifty-first North Carolina, Twelfth and Eighteenth Georgia Battalions, Twentieth Regiment and Seventh Battalion South Carolina, Major James H. Rion commanding. The sortie was made about midnight, driving in the advance picket to the first trench, from which the enemy was drawn; but a heavy fire from a much larger force a hundred or two hundreds yards further on arrested the advance of the assailants, and it was believed killed and wounded a number of the Federal soldiers who were retreating. From prisoners taken it was ascertained that batteries were in course of construction and many guns already mounted. The Confederates lost eleven wounded, one mortally, and three missing. Major Rion estimated the Federal loss at not less than forty.

Battery Wagner was a field work made of sand and riveted with turf and palmetto logs. It extended across the islands from the beach on the east to Vincent's Creek on the west, and presented toward the south a bastioned front of about 275 yards. The parapets were very thick and the ditch of moderate depth. The space within the work was from east to west about 200 yards and from north to south varied from 20 to 75 yards. On this space to the west were quarters for officers and men, built of wood, a bomb-proof (capable of sheltering from eight hundred to a thousand men), bomb-proof magazines and heavy traverses.

On July 18 the armament was one 10-inch columbiad, one 32-pounder rifle, one 42-pounder, and two
32-pounder carronades, two naval shell guns and
one 8-inch seacoast howitzer, four smooth-bore 32-
pounders and one 10-inch sea-coast mortar—in all
thirteen—and one light battery. Of those guns only
the single 10-inch columbiad was of much effect
against the monitors. The Federal land batteries
were beyond the range of nearly all of the other
guns in Wagner.

On the morning of the 18th the infantry of the
garrison consisted of the Thirty-first North Carolina, Lieutenant Colonel C. W. Knight command-
ing; Fifty-first North Carolina, Colonel McKethen;
and the Charleston Battalion, Lieutenant Colonel
P. C. Gaillard. The artillery was Captains W. T.
Tatam's and Warren Adams' companies of the
First South Carolina regular infantry, acting as
artillery; Captains J. T. Buckner's and W. J.
Dixon's companies of the Sixty-third Georgia Heavy
Artillery, and Captain De Pass' Light Battery—in
all an aggregate of about seventeen hundred men.
The Charleston Battalion and Fifty-first North
Carolina were assigned to the defense of the parapet
in the order named from the right along the south
front to the gun chamber opposite the door of the
bomb-proof, which was on the left or sea front. The
Thirty-first North Carolina extended along the sea
face from the left of the Fifty-first to the sallyport
toward Battery Gregg. A part of this regiment
(the Thirty-first) was held in reserve on the parade.

Two companies of the Charleston Battalion, Captain Julius A. Blake commanding, were outside of the work guarding the left gorge and sallyport. Two of Captain De Pass' field pieces were also outside of the work on the traverse near the sallyport. Colonel E. B. Harris, chief of engineers, had that day placed a howitzer on the right of the sallyport, outside of the beach, to co-operate with the guns on the left. To avoid the delay, which in a sudden assault might prove fatal, of assembling the men and marching them in military order to their respective posts, every man was instructed individually as to the exact point which he should occupy, and which, on an order to man the parapets, he would be required to gain and hold. All of the artillery was under the general command of Lieutenant Colonel J. C. Simkins, Chief of Artillery.

On the 16th General Gillmore had completed his preparations and was in readiness for the bombardment and assault, but heavy rains deluged his batteries, damaging the ammunition, and obliged him to defer it until the 18th. He had constructed four batteries, and the long list of officers killed in the then recent battle of Gettysburg furnished names for three of them—Reynolds, Weed, and O'Rorke; the other was Battery Hays. They were at distances from Wagner ranging from 1330 to 1920 yards, and mounted thirty-one rifled guns, varying in caliber from 10-pounders to 30-pounders, nine 10-inch and four 8-inch mortars, in all forty-four pieces. Lieutenant Colonel R. W. Jackson, First United States Artillery, commanded Batteries Hays and

O'Rorke; Captain L. L. Langon, of the same regiment, commanded Batteries Reynolds and Weed.

The naval vessels in readiness to take part in the bombardment were the *New Ironsides,* Captain Rowan, and five monitors, namely the *Kaatskill,* Captain G. W. Rodgers; *Montauk,* Captain D. McN. Fairfax; *Nantucket,* Captain Beaumont; *Weehawken,* Captain Colhoun, and *Patapsco,* Captain Badger. The *Ironsides* carried fourteen and the monitors two guns each, all of 15-inch and 11-inch caliber—the heaviest guns in use. There were besides five gunboats, the *Paul Jones,* Commander Rhind; *Ottawa,* Commander Whiting; *Seneca,* Commander Gibson; *Chippewa,* Commander Harris, and *Wissahickon,* Commander Davis.

General Gillmore had ordered the firing to commence at day dawn on the 18th, but another heavy rain on the night of the 17th delayed it a few hours. About 8:30 A. M. fire was opened, which, until midday, Gillmore says, was merely to obtain the proper range, but the Confederate generals represent it as rapid and heavy from the commencement. About mid-day the land and naval batteries, about ninety guns, were in rapid action and were replied to from batteries on Morris, James, and Sullivan's island and Fort Sumter. The bombardment—rarely, if ever, exceeded in the history of war for the number and caliber of the guns and the rapidity and accuracy of fire—continued until nearly eight o'clock.

Words fail to convey an adequate idea of that bombardment when "the whole island smoked like

a furnace and trembled as from an earthquake."
None but those who witnessed can appreciate it.   To
those who directed the storm "the spectacle presented was of surpassing sublimity and grandeur,"
as described by General Gillmore. But only the
men who were in Wagner on that memorable day
can form an idea of its diabolical power as it appeared to them, which seemed capable of blasting
and destroying everything before it save the indomitable will and resolution of those who defended
the work.

For eleven hours the air seemed filled with every
description of shot and shell that the magazines of
war could supply.   Huge clouds of sand were blown
into the air from the craters formed by the bursting
shells; the water of the bay was lashed into foam
and thrown high in jets of spray by the ricocheting
shots from the ironclads bounding from the water
over the parapets and bursting within the work,
while a dense cloud of sulphurous smoke hung like a
pall over the scene. Of the garrison only the gun
detachments and a few sentinels were at their posts.
The troops generally were ordered to shelter themselves in the bomb-proofs and behind the parapets, traverses, and sand hills. The Charleston
battalion preferred the open air to the stifling heat
and vitiated.atmosphere of the bomb-proof, and
during the whole of that terrible day sheltered themselves as they best could outside. It was necessary
to husband their strength to repel the expected assault. In the meantime their strength was to sit
still.

The 10-inch columbiad, the only gun which could reach the ironclads with effect, and several other guns were soon dismounted and the 32-pounder rifle was rendered useless by bursting. In truth, the armament of Wagner was so inferior to those which opposed it that it was inappreciable. The field and shell guns were dismounted and protected by sand-bags until they should be needed to repel the assault. Comparatively passive endurance alone remained for the garrison while the storm continued. Since the assault of the 11th Wagner had been much strengthened under the skillful direction of the Chief Engineer, Colonel D. B. Harris, and his able assistant, Captain Barnwell, and had stood the severe test of the heavy fire to which it had been subjected so well as to inspire the troops with confidence in the efficacy of sand batteries.

Charleston was wild with excitement. From church steeples, house-tops, and the wharves, from boats in the harbor and the parapets of the surrounding forts and batteries, thousands of eager spectators gazed anxiously on the work which held its gallant defenders, whom they were powerless to assist. Wagner itself exhibited scarcely any sign of life.

The Confederate flag floated defiantly over it, and when the halyards were cut by a shot and the flag was blown into the fort Captain Barnwell, of the Engineers, instantly sprang to the ramparts with a battle-flag and drove the staff into the sand, while others of the garrison leaped forward in a race through the storm of shot and shell for the garrison

flag—Major Ramsey, Sergeant Shelton, and Pro-
vost Flinn, of the Charleston Battalion, and Lieutenant Riddic, of the Sixty-third Georgia, dividing
the honor of flying it again from its staff. It was
again shot away and again restored to its place, this
time by Private Gaillard, of the Charleston Battalion. "These intrepid actions," says General
Taliaferro, "emulating in a higher degree the conduct of Sergeant Jasper at Moultrie, during the
Revolution, were loudly cheered by the command
and inspired them with renewed courage."

While the bombardment was at its height the
Chief of Engineers, Colonel D. B. Harris, a graduate of West Point, of the class of 1833, landed at
Cumming's Point, passed through the tempest of
shot to Wagner to inspect its condition and to give
his personal attention to whatever might be done to
repair the ravages of the bombardment. The perfectly cool courage which characterized him and was
the admiration of all who saw him under the
heaviest fire inspirited the garrison and gave confidence in its capacity to withstand the terrible fire it
was undergoing.

A little more than a year later General Harris
died at Summerville of yellow fever, contracted
while inspecting the defenses of Charleston, leaving
an enviable reputation for skill, patriotism, and intrepid bravery, tempered by a kindly, gentle, and
modest bearing.

The long midsummer day seemed endless and
the storm of fire increased as the hours wore on.
The fierce July sun seemed to stand still. Would

it never set? Water was scarce and men slaked
their thirst from the temporary wells opened by exploding shells into which water oozed. Men were
found dead without wounds from the concussion of
bursting shells. A staff officer, Captain Tuiggs, in
the execution of an order was knocked down by an
exploding shell and found apparently lifeless, with
no wound. He was with difficulty restored. Men
were half buried in sand thrown up by bursting
shells; the commanding general himself was buried
knee deep and dug out with spades.

Much anxiety was felt for the safety of the magazine. The works might be battered out of shape,
the parapet, traverses, scarp, and counterscarp
might be cut down, but the sand could not be
wholly removed and would still afford some shelter;
but if the covering of the magazine were swept
away, a shell bursting would blow the whole garrison skyward. The closest watch was kept upon it
and its condition reported at short intervals during
the day.

Later in the day General Gillmore signaled Admiral Dahlgren to redouble his fire and cease a little
after sunset, when the assault would be made.
Colonel Olmstead, of the First Georgia, who had
been relieved from duty in Wagner in the night of
the 17th and witnessed the bombardment from Fort
Johnson, says the General's signal to the Admiral
was intercepted by a Confederate signal officer, who
knew the Federal signals, and that the dispatch was
known by General Beauregard almost as soon as by
the Admiral; but General Taliaferro has no recollec-

tion that it was communicated to him.   No signal was needed to warn him of the approaching assault.   When the storm of fire culminated about sunset and gradually subsided, it was evident that the supreme hour of the day had come and that the assault was at hand.   Orders were given to man the ramparts; the field guns and howitzers were unearthed and mounted, and all preparations made to meet and repel the assault.

General Gillmore had selected the time between sunset and dark to make the assault, in order that there might be light enough for his troops to see their way, but not enough to enable the gunners in the distant Confederate batteries to see distinctly the advancing column.   General Seymour commanded in person the division of troops available for the assault.   It had been suggested to him—he does not say by whom—that one brigade would be sufficient for the work in hand, but Seymour thought differently.   On close personal observation of Wagner he could not discover that it had been materially damaged by the unprecedentedly heavy bombardment to which it had been subjected, but he presumed that so heavy a fire must have in a great measure demoralized the garrison.

The First Brigade—General G. C. Strong's— was selected to lead the assault.   It was composed of the Fifty-fourth Massachusetts Regiment, Colonel Shaw; the Sixth Connecticut, Colonel Chatfield; a battalion of the Seventh Connecticut, Captain Gray; the Forty-eighth New York, Colonel Barton; the Third New Hampshire, Colonel Jack-

son; Ninth Maine, Colonel Emery, and Seventy-
sixth Pennsylvania, Captain J. S. Little commanding. It was supported by Colonel H. S. Putnam's
Brigade, composed of his own regiment, the Seventh
New Hampshire, Lieutenant Colonel Abbott; One
Hundredth New York, Colonel Dandy; Sixty-
second Ohio, Colonel Pond, and Sixty-seventh Ohio,
Colonel Voris. General Stevenson's Brigade of
four excellent regiments was held in reserve.

The First Brigade was formed in column by
regiments, except the Fifty-fourth Massachusetts,
which being much larger than the others, numbering nearly a thousand men, was in column by battalion. It was a negro regiment, recruited in
Massachusetts, and was regarded as an admirable
and reliable body of men. Half the ground to be
traversed before reaching Wagner was undulating
with sand hills, which afforded some shelter, but
not so much as to prevent free and easy movement;
the other half smooth and unobstructed up to the
ditch. Within easy range of Wagner the marsh
encroached so much on the firm sand of the island
as to leave but a narrow way between it and the
water. A few stirring words were addressed by the
officers to their troops and the men responded with
cheers.

About half-past seven the assaulting column was
hurled against Wagner, with orders to use the
bayonet only, the Federal artillery continuing their
fire over their heads as long as it could be done
without risk to their own men. The Confederates
at their posts were straining their eyes to catch

through the deepening twilight the first glimpse of the enemy. When the head of the column came in view a rapid fire of grape and canister was opened, and the fire from James' Island batteries was poured in on the flank. Sumter and Gregg, firing over Wagner, plunged their shot into the advancing column and the parapets of Wagner were lit up by a line of infantry fire.

The advancing column pressed defiantly forward, breasting the storm of iron and lead which was rapidly thinning their ranks. The leading regiment, the Fifty-fourth Massachusetts, was soon thrown into a state of disorder, which reacted injuriously on those which followed. The wounded "and many unhurt" were hastening in crowds from the front along the beach. So heavy was the fire and so great the disorder that General Seymour saw the necessity of immediate support, and accordingly dispatched his Assistant Inspector General, Major Plympton, of the Third New Hampshire, to order up Colonel Putnam with his supporting brigade. To his amazement Colonel Putnam positively refused to advance, because, as he explained, he had been ordered by General Gillmore to remain where he was.

In the meantime the First Brigade was urged on with admirable spirit and gallantry by General Strong, who had been assured of prompt support. But the destructive fire from Wagner was more than his men could stand. The Fifty-fourth Massachusetts broke and fled, large bodies of it falling upon and with violence forcing their way through the ranks of the advancing column, greatly heightening the general confusion. The First Brigade had, indeed, ceased for the time to be an organized body and came surging back to the rear in confusion.

General Strong had urged his command on with great spirit and gallantry, but his losses had been so severe that his regiments were much shaken, and the consequent confusion was much heightened by the yielding of the leading regiment, portions of which fell harshly upon those in the rear. Fragments of each regiment, however, brave men bravely led, went eagerly over the ditch, mounted the parapet, and struggled with the foe inside. But their efforts were too feeble to affect the contest materially.

The storm of fire from Wagner had strewn the ditch and glacis with killed and wounded. A few of the bravest of the different regiments, notably the Forty-eighth New York and Sixth Connecticut, continued to press forward, bearing their colors and striving to reach the ditch and mount the parapet; but the brigade had been hopelessly repulsed, its gallant commander, General Strong, was mortally wounded, as was Colonel Chatfield. Colonel Shaw, of the Fifty-fourth Massachusettes, was killed, and many other officers killed and wounded. The mass of the brigade was hastening in disorder to the shelter of the sand hills and trenches.

What were Colonel Putnam's feelings in the meantime perhaps will never be known, but may with much certainty be conjectured. He was a gallant young officer and could not stand idly by at the head of a fine brigade and see the command of his classmates and intimate friends cut to pieces. "After a disastrous delay and without orders," says General Seymour, "he led his brigade forward and pressed on to the assault of the southeast angle through a destructive fire, for, the first brigade having been repulsed, the fire from the center and both flanks of Wagner were crossed in front of that angle, sweeping the glacis and ditch with fatal effect."

It seems that the terrible bombardment of eleven hours had demoralized the Thirty-first North Carolina Regiment. It did not respond to the call to man the ramparts. The southeast bastion and sea front, to the defense of which it had been assigned, was therefore unguarded. Colonel Putnam and a part of his brigade crossed the ditch, which had been nearly filled with sand by the long bombardment, mounted the parapet, and a hundred or more men gained possession of the southeast bastion.

Seeing the advantage gained by Colonel Putnam, General Seymour had just dispatched an order by Major Plympton to General Stevenson to advance with his brigade to Colonel Putnam's support, when he, too, was severely wounded. Before he was carried from the field he repeated the order to General Stevenson to advance, but the order was not obeyed. Why does not appear.

Colonel Putnam, surrounded by his chief officers —Colonel Dandy, One Hundredth New York; Major Butler, Sixty-seventh Ohio; Major Coan, Forty-eighth New York; Captain Klein, Sixth Connecticut, and others—was encouraging his men to hold the ground they had gained, assuring them that they would soon be reinforced, when he was shot dead, "as brave a soldier, as courteous a gentleman, as true a man as ever walked beneath the Stars and Stripes," says his division commander. An officer of his staff—Lieutenant Cate, Seventh New Hampshire—seeing the Colonel fall, sprang to his side to aid him, when he, too, was struck by a shot and fell dead across the body of his chief.

The Federal loss had been heavy, especially in officers of rank. When General Seymour was taken from the field wounded, General Gillmore sent forward his chief of staff, General Turner, to assume command and draw off the troops. Those not already within the work, despairing of support, retreated as rapidly as they could through a destructive fire until they gained the shelter of the sand hills and trenches.

Those who had effected an entrance could not escape through the cross fire in their rear and would not surrender. The assailants had become the assailed. Volunteers were called for from the garrison to overcome and capture them. Major McDonald, of the Fifty-first North Carolina, and Captain Ryan, of the Charleston Battalion, quickly sprang forward for the service. The latter with his company was selected; the captain was shot dead at the moment of the charge, his men faltered and the opportunity was lost.

The desperate men inside seemed resolved to sell their lives dearly rather than surrender. General

Hagood had arrived with Colonel Harrison's regiment, the Thirty-second Georgia, to reinforce the garrison. That regiment was sent along the parapet to the left and on the top of the magazine and approached the rear of the imprisoned Federals, who, seeing themselves so greatly outnumbered and with no hope of escape, laid down their arms.[1]

The repulse was complete and disastrous. General Seymour attributes the failure of the assault "solely to the unfortunate delay that hindered Colonel Putnam from moving promptly in obedience to my orders, and to his not being supported after he had essentially succeeded in the assault." The heavy losses of the assailants attest their daring and determined resolution, and their division commander awards them the highest praise for the gallantry with which they "did their full duty that night."

The light of the next morning disclosed a ghastly scene of slaughter. The ditch and ground in front of Wagner were thickly strewn with killed and wounded.

The Confederate loss was only 174; surprisingly

[1]Major Lewis Butler, of the Sixty-seventh Ohio, who was by the side of Colonel Putman when the latter was killed, says: "It is but just that I notice a special order of General Beauregard, under date of July 27, 1863 (if I am correct as to date), directing that special care be taken of the wounded captured at Wagner, as men who were brave enough to go in there deserved the respect of their enemies. Another act of courtesy: The effects, money, and papers belonging to members of the Sixty-seventh Ohio Volunteer Infantry who died in Charleston Hospital were sent through the lines by flag of truce."

small, thanks to the sheltering capacity of sand works. The loss on both sides had been unusually heavy in commissioned officers. Among the Confederate killed were Lieutenant Colonel J. C. Simkins, First South Carolina Infantry; Captain W. H. Ryan, of the Charleston Battalion; Captain W. T. Tatam, First South Carolina Infantry, and Lieutenant G. W. Thompson, commanding company, Fifty-first North Carolina. Major David Ramsay, of the Charleston Battalion, was severely wounded. Lieutenant Colonel Simkins, as Chief of Artillery, had directed the operations of that arm with admirable skill and daring, and when the assault commenced mounted the parapet to aid and encourage the infantry. "There on the ramparts in the front this admirable soldier and accomplished gentleman sealed his devotion to our cause by an early but most heroic death."

The Federal loss has never been officially ascertained. General Taliaferro estimated it at not less than 2000, perhaps much more. General Beauregard in his official report says their loss must have been 3000, as 800 bodies were interred in front of Battery Wagner on the following morning.

In a letter of the 20th to Admiral Dahlgren General Gillmore tells that during the ten days from the beginning of his operations he had lost thirty-three per cent. of his troops in killed, wounded, missing, and sick. He had commenced with somewhat more than 13,000 on Morris and Folly islands, and his tri-monthly report for the 20th of

July shows an aggregate sick on those two islands of 1241. It would seem therefore that General Beauregard's estimate was not excessive.

General Hagood relieved General Taliaferro in command of Wagner on the morning of the 19th. The latter had been in command since the 13th, and he and the officers and men of his command received the highest encomiums from Generals Beauregard and Ripley for skill and gallantry in the defense of this important post. The Fifty-first North Carolina had brilliantly sustained the honor of their State, and was highly commended, especially the field officers, Colonel McKethen, Lieutenant Colonel C. B. Hobson, and Major McDonald. The next year in the operations around Petersburg the Thirty-first North Carolina wiped out the reproach it had incurred in a terrible moment of weakness. Sunday, July 19, passed quietly and was devoted under a flag of truce to burying the dead and caring for the wounded.

The next day the bombardment was renewed from both land and naval batteries. The Admiral suggested to the General to advance his batteries and renew the assault by columns advancing simultaneously on the southern and northern fronts. General Gillmore demurred, because the attempt would involve too heavy a loss of life for his already greatly reduced force. He agreed, however, to make another assault, provided the Admiral would furnish from his fleet the column to assail the work from the north, a proposal which the Admiral promptly declined. The policy of carrying Wagner by assault was therefore abandoned and the science of engineering resorted to. The object which the assaulting columns had failed to effect it was decided to attain by the slower process of a regular siege.

CHAPTER XII

Referring to Battery Wagner, Major General
Gillmore says in the official report of his operations
on Morris Island: "The nature of its construction
demanded and enticed an actual attempt upon the
works to make manifest its real and concealed ele-
ments of strength." He had on two occasions yielded
to its enticements to attack first on the morning of
the 11th and again on the evening of the 18th of
July, 1863, and the results had been disastrous on
both occasions, especially on the evening of July 18,
when the assault had signally failed with a loss in
his command variously estimated at from 1600 to
3000 men, among their killed being General G. C.
Strong and Colonel H. S. Putnam, commanding the
two brigades which made the assault, and Colonels
J. L. Chatfield and R. G. Shaw, commanding regiments.

Battery Wagner had exhibited such formidable
strength in itself, and its gallant commanders on
both occasions, General William B. Taliaferro and
Colonel Graham, and the officers and men under

their command such skill and resolution in utilizing
that strength to its utmost, as convinced General Gillmore that the work could not be carried by assault,
even with the aid of the most powerful land and
naval batteries ever brought to bear upon so small
an object without a greater sacrifice of men than
he was disposed to make. He did indeed assent
to a suggestion made by Admiral Dahlgren to renew
the assault with columns advancing simultaneously
on the north and south fronts of the battery, but
only on the condition that the Admiral should furnish from his fleet the column to assault the northern
front. He had, he said, lost one-third of his command in killed, wounded, captured and sick during
the ten days' operations on Morris Island. Another
assault would involve a heavier loss of life than his
already greatly reduced force alone could bear. The
Admiral declined to furnish an assaulting column
from his fleet, which had also a fearfully large sick
list.

The plan, therefore, of carrying Battery Wagner
by assault was abandoned and the longer and more
tedious process of reducing it scientifically by regular
approaches was adopted. The contest for the possession of Morris Island lapsed therefore into one
of engineering skill and steady endurance. With
sufficient labor, long-range guns, and other necessary
material the prospect of a successful defense would
have been encouraging—without them it was hopeless. The wealth of material and all manner of
necessary appliances for siege operations on the
Federal so greatly exceeded that of the Confederate

side that the ultimate result was never for a moment doubtful. From the moment that General Gillmore secured so firm a foothold on Morris Island that General Beauregard felt and acknowledged his inability to dislodge him, the ultimate occupation of the whole island was only a question of time.

Charleston was General Gillmore's objective point, which he proposed to gain by way of Morris Island and the subsequent action of the fleet. For the complete success of his plan it was exceedingly important that he should, with the least possible delay, demolish Fort Sumter and silence Fort Moultrie and other batteries on the west of Sullivan's Island, the accomplishment of which formed a part of his plan, and thus open the gate to Charleston for the entrance of the fleet before his adversary could prepare other works to bar his approach to the city. Every hour's delay was important to the Confederates, which gave them time to prepare interior works of defense.

In that view of the case it would seem that in an affair of so much moment, instead of relying upon two brigades, or one, as General Seymour intimates that General Gillmore did, to carry Battery Wagner by assault on the evening of July 18, it would have been better in a humane, as well as a military point of view, if General Gillmore had on that occasion hurled his whole available force against it, or even to have renewed the assault as soon as his shattered columns could have been re-formed and brought up to the work and before reinforcements could arrive. That course might, perhaps, have resulted in the capture of Wagner. The loss would probably not have been greater than that which resulted from the daily tale of killed and wounded in the trenches and the heavier loss by disease attending the fifty days' siege which followed, and the physical suffering would have been less.

It had been deemed essential to the success of General Gillmore's plan of operations that his force should occupy the whole of Morris Island before proceeding to demolish Fort Sumter and silence the Sullivan's Island works. To gain possession of the island involved the necessity of capturing Batteries Wagner and Gregg. Ten days' experience on the island had demonstrated that the reduction of the two batteries would require a much longer time than had been supposed.

General Gillmore was amply supplied with means, and though untrammeled by instructions from his government he was under a strong pressure of public opinion and expectation to hasten forward his operations. He had been selected by President Lincoln for this important service, on which he had entered on the urgent recommendation of the most distinguished and influential journalist of that day in this country, and had staked his professional reputation on the accomplishment of the task he had undertaken. There were, besides, newspaper correspondents with his command to prick him on to action, if necessary, and to keep the public informed of the progress of the operations for the capture of Charleston. To gain time, therefore, he somewhat modified his original plan of operations and decided to attempt the demolition of Fort Sumter with bat-teries, to be established on ground already in his possession, firing over Wagner and Gregg.

The conception and execution of this plan of operations strikingly illustrates the marvelous pro-gress that had been made in a year or so in the manufacture of heavy ordnance. About fifteen months earlier it had been thought wonderful that breaching batteries at the distance of a mile had reduced Fort Pulaski at the mouth of the Savannah River. Now at more than double the distance it was proposed to reduce Fort Sumter. Nothing in siege operations approaching it had ever been known.

Immediately after the repulse of the assaulting columns on the evening of July 18, and while hun-dreds of his killed and wounded were lying on the ground where they had fallen in front of Wagner, General Gillmore gave orders for converting the positions occupied by his most advanced batteries into a strong defensive line capable of withstanding the most formidable attack his adversary could prob-ably make against it, and for the erection of breach-ing batteries against Fort Sumter.

Probably no besieging army was ever better equipped for the work to be done than was that which General Gillmore commanded. In addition to a corps of skillful engineer and artillery officers, there was in his command an admirable and most useful engineer regiment—the First New York En-gineers. The Colonel, E. W. Serrell, and many of the officers were practical engineers. The enlisted men were picked and many of them skilled mechanics, who were of incalculable service, not only for the actual labor they performed, but for their capacity to instruct and direct others in all the mechanical work incident to a siege. And although the ground was in many respects exceedingly unfavorable for offensive engineering operations, presenting as it did much too narrow a front, and being in some places subject to overflow in stormy weather, these drawbacks were more than counterbalanced by the presence of a powerful fleet immediately on the right flank, within easy and effective range, and always ready to aid and sustain the operations on land by its heavy and accurate fire. Unquestionably Admiral Dahlgren's fleet contributed greatly to the success of the operations on land. Indeed, it is not probable that the plan of operations by way of Morris Island would ever have been undertaken without the certainty of the naval co-operation, or if undertaken without such co-operation they would probably have failed, General Gillmore's opinion to the contrary notwithstanding.

Anticipating the damaging effect on Fort Sumter of the enemy's heavy rifled guns firing from stationary batteries on Morris Island, General Beauregard had early commenced and continued nightly a partial disarmament of that fort, removing all long-range guns that could be spared to be mounted elsewhere on interior lines. He instructed General Ripley, who commanded the military district embracing the scene of operations, to strengthen the gorge wall south face of Sumter on the interior by bales of cotton kept damp, the space between them to be filled in with sand-bags, and also to place a covering of sand-bags on the scarp wall of the same face from bottom to top, if possible, and to protect the guns remaining in the fort by traverse and merlons.

The armament of Battery Wagner was slightly increased; so was that of Fort Johnson. Fort Moultrie and Battery Bee were to be connected by a covered way, and orders were given to press rapidly to completion the new works on Shell Point (called Battery Simkins in honor of the gallant Colonel of that name who fell on the parapet of Wagner during the assault of July 18), and Batteries Chevers and Haskel in close proximity to it. General Beauregard's plan, briefly stated, was to establish a circle of batteries from Legare's Point on Schooner Creek, James Island, to Battery Beauregard, on Sullivan's Island, so as to concentrate their fire, including that of Sumter and Moultrie, on the northern half of Morris Island, to retard the siege operations and to overwhelm or harass the enemy so soon as he should gain full possession of that island.

The attack and defense were both conducted with admirable and determined courage. It was a species of warfare most trying to the patience and endurance of the troops engaged, and for which it might have been supposed new troops were least adapted. Many consecutive days and nights the monotonous work went on, exposing the men to the perils without the excitement of battle. While the heavy guns on each side were actively employed to retard and demolish the works of the other, skillful marksmen, armed with the longest range rifles, were employed in efforts to pick off the gunners, and the daily reports of the progress of the works were as regularly accompanied by the reports of the killed and wounded in accomplishing it. Whenever the Confederate fire became so galling—as it often did —that work on the trenches and batteries could not be continued without too heavy a sacrifice of life and limb, a signal from the General to the Admiral would send a monitor or so abreast of Wagner, and a storm of iron and lead would be thrown into the work, which generally ended in driving the garrison, with the exception of the necessary gunners and sentinels, to the cover of the bomb-proof until the fire from the ironclads should cease. But the heaviest fire could not wholly suppress the fire of the sharpshooters, who had become exceedingly expert in covering themselves in the sand hills and with sand-bags.

The greater part of the work was done under cover of the darkness of night, interrupted occasionally when the bright harvest moon would light up the scene. A most unpleasant and revolting part of the work in the trenches was the removal of the dead bodies—sometimes as many as ten in a night— of those who had been killed by the sharpshooters, which the sappers, while prosecuting their work, disturbed in their graves. At first these bodies were moved and reburied out of the way, as was supposed, but the exigencies of the engineering operations demanded all the space not covered by marsh, and it soon became necessary to disturb again and again their dead comrades, until the attempt to rebury them beyond reach was abandoned, and in future when the graves were encountered the bodies were built with mother earth into the parapets and there left.

By the evening of August 16 the third parallel had been completed and twelve batteries erected and made ready for action. Those especially intended for the bombardment of Sumter were at an average distance from that fort of 3917 yards—the nearest being 3428 and the most remote 4290 yards. The twelve batteries mounted twenty-eight heavy rifles of calibers from 32- to 300-pounders, and twelve 10-inch mortars; in all forty pieces. One of them, called the "Naval Battery," mounting two 8-inch Parrott rifles and two 80-pounder Whitworth rifles, was manned by sailors from the United States frigate *Wabash* and commanded by Captain Foxhall A. Parker, United States Navy. The others were manned by the Third Rhode Island Heavy Artillery and detachments from the One Hundredth and One Hundred and Seventy-eighth New York, the Seventh Connecticut, and Eleventh Maine Infantry, and Company C, First United States Artillery.

The positions occupied by the Federal troops were thoroughly protected by defensive works and covered by inclined palisading and wire entanglements stretching entirely across the island. Provision was made for sweeping the fronts of the defensive works by the fire of eight field guns and several Requa batteries. The latter were novelties in warfare, and consisted each of twenty-five rifle barrels, so adjusted on a frame as to deliver a diffused fan-shaped fire of 175 shots a minute, and it was claimed were effective at the distance of a mile or more. The Federal position on Morris Island was thus made as secure against an assault as was Battery Wagner itself.

Fort Sumter, against which these powerful breaching and mortar batteries were to be directed, was at that time commanded by the same officer, Colonel Alfred Rhett, of the First South Carolina Artillery, aided by Major Ormsby Blanding, of the same regiment, who had so gallantly and successfully defended it on April 7 against the ironclad attack and the fort was garrisoned as then by men of his own regiment. About day dawn on the morning of August 17 the land batteries opened on Sumter, directing the fire of the rifles or breaching guns against the gorge wall, the mortars dropping shells into the fort. The ironclads and gunboats soon took up their prescribed positions and joined in the general fire.

Batteries Wagner and Gregg replied with spirit, but for several hours Sumter gave no sign of life, the only object visible about it being the flag which floated over it in the summer breeze. Wagner and Gregg continued the fire, while the fifteen- and eleven-inch shells from the ironclads hurled the sand in cartloads from their parapets. About midday these two batteries ceased firing, and Fort Sumter opened, and so the thunder of heavy guns went on, gradually ceasing as if from exhaustion as the long summer day passed, and the first day's bombardment ended. Nine hundred and forty-eight shots had been fired at

Sumter, and, the fire being surprisingly accurate for the great distance at which it was delivered, the fort was much damaged. The gorge wall had been deeply cut into and other walls badly shaken. One man of the garrison had been killed and Lieutenants John Johnson, of the Engineers, and John Middleton and Julius Rhett, of the First South Carolina Artillery, and ten men wounded.

Usually the monitors performed their part in the bombardments with immunity to life and limb, the officers and men being shielded by an eleven-inch thickness of iron. On this day, however, soon after they had gone into action, the *Kaatskill* was seen steaming away, going southward, a signal from her announcing that her commander, Captain G. W. Rodgers, had been killed. He was the Admiral's chief of staff, and usually accompanied - him into action, but on this occasion he had asked to be allowed to command his monitor, the *Kaatskill*. The action had scarcely commenced when a shot struck the pilot house, forcing off a large piece of iron on the inside, which struck and killed Captain Rodgers and Paymaster John G. Woodbury, who was standing by him, and wounding the pilot and quartermaster. The Admiral speaks in the most complimentary terms of Captains Rodgers' great merit.

Battery Wagner had suffered but little except in the death of its engineer, Captain Wampler. In the midst of the heaviest fire, which had driven the garrison, with the exception of the gunners, sentries, and sharpshooters to the shelter of the bomb-proof, it was discovered that the heavy bombardment had slipped the covering of sand from the principal magazine to such an extent as greatly to endanger the whole garrison. Captain Wampler, with a party of men, hastened to repair the injury, under the destructive fire. In the evening, when it was supposed the firing had ceased for the night, he was sitting with the commanding officer, Colonel Keitt, and Lieutenant Charles S. Hill, ordnance officer, when a shell from the *Ironsides* fell in the midst of them and, bursting, crushed the gallant young officer.

The fire from the breaching batteries continued for seven consecutive days and was incessant from daylight until dark. At the close of the seventh day of the bombardment, the twenty-third day, the destruction of the offensive powers of Fort Sumter seemed complete.

The heavy firing ceased, and though a slow fire was maintained, the bombardment was regarded as having successfully accomplished its purpose. Sumter seemed a shapeless mass of ruins. There was but one gun in the fort that could be fired, and that was a thirty-two pounder smooth-bore, whose only use was to fire the usual evening gun. Within the fort the débris of masonry, broken guns and carriages, cotton bales and sand-bags, ripped and torn to pieces, were mingled in inextricable confusion. General Gillmore reported officially that Fort Sumter was demolished, its offensive powers destroyed, and that it was reduced to the condition of a mere infantry outpost, incapable of retarding the approaches to Battery Wagner or of inflicting injury upon the ironclads. Nevertheless the Confederate flag still floated over the ruins, and the usual evening gun announced that the fort was still occupied.

Now that its batteries were effectually silenced, it had ceased to be an artillery post, and the garrison which had so long and gallantly defended it was withdrawn on the night of September 4, and assigned to other duty, the Charleston Battalion of infantry, Major Julius A. Blake, succeeding the artillery as the garrison of the ruined fort. Major Stephen Elliott succeeded Colonel Rhett in command of Fort Sumter. The latter gentleman had commanded longer than any other officer, and his name, together with that of his regiment, the First South Carolina Regular Artillery, is indissolubly linked with the famous fort they had so long defended with admirable skill and comspicuous gallantry.

General Gillmore regarded his part in the general plan for the capture of Charleston as virtually accomplished when he had succeeded in destroying the offensive power of Fort Sumter, and thus opened the gate to Charleston for the entrance of the ironclad fleet. But during the month of August his command had been reinforced by General George H. Gordon's Division of two brigades (Schimmelfennig's and Ames') and three other brigades, Wild's Foster's, and Alford's, and with the force and material at his command something more than the silencing of Sumter was expected of him. The possession of the whole of Morris Island, including Batteries Wagner and Gregg, he did not regard as essential to the entrance of the fleet into the harbor. Wagner and Gregg were mere outworks auxiliary to the defense of Sumter; the latter having been silenced, the possession of the former was important only as facilitating a stricter blockade of the port. It only remained, so General Gillmore thought and said, for Admiral Dahlgren to perform his part of the general plan, to enter the harbor with his fleet and take possession of the city of Charleston.

The Admiral, however, did not so regard it; indeed, he did not admit that he was a consenting party to any such general plan. He was ready and anxious to enter the harbor when the obstructions in the way should have been removed; but they were not yet removed. There stood Sumter, an obstacle in itself, and protecting other obstacles which the Confederates had placed in the way.

While approaching Wagner and preparing to demolish Sumter, General Gillmore had made other preparations, by which he seems to have supposed that he might gain possession not only of Sumter, but of the whole of Morris Island, without striking another blow. He had with great difficulty and at much cost constructed a battery known as the "Swamp Angel," in the marsh between Morris Island and the Confederate works on James Island, from which Charleston could be bombarded. On August 21 he addressed a letter to General Beauregard demanding the surrender of Fort Sumter and the whole of Morris Island. There was some delay in the delivery of this letter, and when opened it was found to be without signature, and was returned to General Gillmore's headquarters. Of course General Beauregard declined to comply with the extraordinary demand, and a little after midnight the bombardment of Charleston commenced and, it may be added, was continued with varying violence for nearly eighteen months. Fifteen incendiary shells were fired into the city that night from an eight-inch Parrott rifle, destroying some medical stores, but doing little damage to the city.

The indignant refusal of General Beauregard to surrender Fort Sumter and Morris Island, coupled with a reminder that "after two years of trial you have failed to capture this city or its defenses," prompted General Gillmore to attempt at once to seize Sumter by assault. The assaulting party was to consist of six hundred men to be selected by colonels of regiments, and General Ames, commanding a brigade of General Gordon's Division, was selected to command it. He did not purpose to hold Sumter after seizing it, but to blow it up. He was dissuaded, however, from making the assault, the more readily because he had received information which he regarded as reliable, that the Confederates themselves intended to blow up the fort when it should be rendered untenable.

CHAPTER XIII

Operations against Wagner, which had been
somewhat delayed by the bombardment of Sumter, were resumed with redoubled vigor when the
latter work was apparently demolished. Between
two and three hundred yards in front of Wagner
was a sand ridge occupied by Confederate sharpshooters, who greatly annoyed the sappers engaged
in pushing forward the trenches. In conjunction
with the fire from James Island, Wagner, and Gregg
they occasionally interrupted entirely the work in
the trenches. On the evening of August 21 the One
Hundredth New York, Colonel Dandy, made a
dash to drive them off, but was repulsed. All of
the lighter mortars were then moved up to the
front to dislodge them by a vertical fire, but that
attempt also failed. The Union engineer officers in
charge reported that while the efficiency of the Confederate sharpshooters was daily increasing, their
own was falling off, and that for the further prosecution of the work it was absolutely essential that

the Confederates should be driven off or captured and the ridge occupied by Union troops.

On the 26th General Gillmore placed the resources of the command at the disposal of General Terry, who was in immediate command, with orders to dislodge those sharpshooters at the point of the bayonet and hold the ridge. Between six and seven that evening the Twenty-fourth Massachusetts, Lieutenant Colonel F. A. Osborne, supported by the Third New Hampshire, Captain I. F. Randlett, were thrown upon the ridge and readily occupied it, capturing seventy-six of the eighty-nine men of the Sixty-first North Carolina Regiment, which constituted the whole picket line. The fourth parallel was immediately marked out and constructed on that ridge within two hundred and fifty yards of Wagner.

The darkest and gloomiest days of the siege were now at hand. The exceedingly narrow front of approach, in one place scarcely more than twenty-five yards at high tide, gave great effect to the direct and flank fire on the head of the sap. The way was over ground defended by torpedoes, which were designed to explode by the tread of persons passing over them, or by the chance strokes of the picks and shovels in the hands of the sappers. "Here is a log in my way," said a sapper to the officer who was directing the work.. "Never mind, dig around it," was the reply, and the next instant the supposed log exploded, blowing the sapper to pieces.

The losses in the trenches were increasing from day to day and the progress was discouragingly slow and uncertain. The sick list was fearfully large; so large that it is said the chief surgeon had advised that the work be again assaulted and the siege ended at the point of the bayonet, as involving a probable less loss of life than the slow process of regular approaches was inflicting on the command. The returns of the Union forces for August show a sick list of 4661 in an aggregate force present of 29,405, and for September of 5269 in an aggregate of 28,981. About the middle of August the sick list was nearly one-fourth of the aggregate force present.

"Matters indeed seemed at a standstill," says General Gillmore, "and a feeling of despondency began to pervade the rank and file of the command. There seemed, indeed, no adequate return to accomplished results for the daily losses which we suffered and no means of relief cheering and encouraging to the soldiers appeared near at hand."

No wonder that there was gloom and despondency among the rank and file, when it had long since begun to dawn upon officers high in rank, and had strengthened into conviction, that possession of the whole of the little sandbank would be but a lamentably inadequate return for the expenditure of so much labor, treasure, health, and life. Public sentiment at the North clamored for the destruction of Sumter and the capture of Charleston. The sentiment which demanded the destruction of Sumter had been gratified when General Gillmore reported that the fort had been demolished and reduced to a mere infantry outpost, but the Union forces were practically no nearer to Charleston than when the campaign opened. The question naturally suggested itself, Would the possession of Wagner really bring them any nearer to the objective point? And with many the answer was emphatically No! It seemed that the siege must be abandoned or new life and vigor thrown into it.

General Gillmore determined to pursue the latter course. Wagner should be overwhelmed by the heaviest fire from land and naval batteries, driving the men to the shelter of the bomb-proofs and keeping them there, while the heaviest rifle guns should pound and demolish the bomb-proofs and so uncover and expose the garrison to the heaviest fire that had yet been thrown against it. In the meantime the sap should be pressed forward to the ditch and the fort stormed and carried at the point of the bayonet, if the stubborn garrison would not surrender before that last resort became necessary.

As preliminary to the complete success of these final operations, General Gillmore proposed to surprise and seize Battery Gregg, thus at once cutting off reinforcements for Wagner and the escape of the garrison.

The attempt was made on the night of the 4th by troops in barges, supported by naval boats, armed with howitzers. All was in readiness soon after dark except one boat, which, having pulled out further toward Sumter than the others, discovered a small Confederate boat, which happened just at that time to be carrying to Charleston Major W. F. Waley, of the Second South Carolina Artillery, who had been badly wounded that day. The officer in charge of the Union boat could not resist the temptation to capture the Confederate, gave chase, and fired upon it. He succeeded in capturing the boat and the wounded officer, but the firing had aroused the garrison of Gregg, disclosed the surprise party, and defeated the expedition. It was attempted again the next night, but it could scarcely have been expected that a garrison which had so narrowly escaped a formidable surprise attack on the preceding night would not be on the alert. If there was any such expectation General Gillmore effectually defeated it himself. In the afternoon of the 5th he signaled Admiral Dahlgren: "I shall try Cummings' Point to-night and want the sailors again early. Will you please send in two or three monitors just by dark to open fire on Moultrie as a diversion? The last time they were in they stopped reinforcements and may do it to-night. Don't want any fire in the rear from reinforcements. The signal for assault will be the hauling down of the red light on the *Ironsides*. I shall display skirmishers behind Wagner and Gregg. Don't fire into them; let the *Ironsides* engage—by nine o'clock."

This dispatch was intercepted by a Confederate signal officer and forwarded to General Ripley, who communicated it to Colonel Keitt, commanding Wagner, with instructions to him to prepare to repel the attack.

Major James Gardner, commanding the Twenty seventh Georgia Infantry, already supporting Gregg, was warned of the impending attack and reinforced after dark by seventy men of the Twenty-fifth South Carolina Infantry and two field howitzers, manned from Kanapaux's Light Artillery, Lieutenant Macbeth commanding, and directed to prepare to repel the attack. The beach between Wagner and Gregg was picketed by 50 men of the Twenty-eighth Georgia. At ten o'clock Major Gardner reported that his whole force numbered only 234 men—too small for the work required of it, but added: "I shall hold the place if it is possible."

The monitors were promptly in position and swept with their fire the ground between the two forts; but there was confusion in assembling the barges in position and so much delay that it was past midnight before the assault was attempted, when Captain Lesesne, commanding Battery Gregg, discovered fifteen or twenty barges approaching from the junction of Vincent and Schooner creeks with muffled oars. He waited until they approached to within about one hundred and seventy yards, when he opened upon them with ten-inch canister. Fort Moultrie also opened fire, sweeping the water on both sides of Cummings' Point.

The fire produced a panic among the assaliants, who had expected to surprise the post. Some of the boats were turned back and pulled rapidly away; others were pulled toward the beach, some men in them crying out not to fire, that they were friends, but they were answered by a fire from the infantry and the field howitzers. All these turned and were pulled rapidly back through the creeks and marshes with serious loss in killed and wounded, the troops generally dispirited by the failure of the expedition.

In this affair Captain J. R. Haines, of the Twenty-eighth Georgia, and Lieutenant R. A. Blum, of the Twenty-fifth South Carolina, were killed by a shell from a monitor.

At dawn on the 5th the final bombardment of Wagner commenced, and for forty-two consecutive hours seventeen mortars and twenty-four rifled guns —one hundred-, two hundred-, and three hundred-pounders—and the guns of the *New Ironsides* poured an incessant fire of shot and shell night and day on the battery. The heavy rifle fire was directed against the southeast angle of the bomb-proof for the purpose of demolishing it and exposing the garrison to the vertical fire of the mortars and the *Ironsides*. The ricochet fire of the ironclads was especially effective. Long practice had given the gunners great accuracy of aim and their eleven-inch shells, bounding gracefully from the water, leaped over the parapet and, bursting within, searched the doomed work in every part. At Wagner night was turned into day. Calcium lights thrown on the fort brilliantly lighted it, bringing out every object in vivid and sharp relief, while the besiegers were shrouded in impenetrable darkness.

Under this overpowering fire the trenches were pressed forward rapidly and almost with impunity, for the sappers were so near Wagner that the distant batteries on James and Sullivan's islands could not fire upon them without risk of dropping their shot into the fort. With the exception of an occasional telling fire from the sharpshooters, Wagner itself was almost as silent as the grave. At the

first shot from the *Ironsides* nearly all of the infantry not already in the sandhills between Wagner
and Gregg were ordered into the bomb-proof, leaving a few sentinels and sharpshooters at the parapet.
Full detachments of artillerymen were kept at the
guns on the land front. It would have been a useless waste of life to keep men exposed to that
storm of shot and shell. The best that could be
done was to husband all resources to repel the assault which was anticipated.

Life in the bomb-proof during the forty-two hours
of the bombardment had become almost unen-
durable. The men were crowded together in the
dark place, where the surgeons were occasionally
obliged to operate on the wounded by the dim light
of a candle. Some men fainted and others were
exhausted by breathing the hot, vitiated atmosphere;
if a man stepped out for an instant to catch a breath
of fresh air he did so at the peril of his life. The
men who had been killed in the two assaults had been
buried, the Federals in front and the Confederates
in rear of Wagner. The graves were necessarily
shallow and in shifting sand. The besiegers had
been burrowing through the graves, removing the
bodies. The ground had been torn up in every
direction by nearly two months' firing and the wind
had blown off the sand, exposing corpses to the
fierce summer sun, tainting and poisoning the air.
Even the water in the shallow wells within the fort
was so tainted as to be unfit for use, and the garrison had to rely upon the precarious supply that
could be brought from Charleston.

The effect of the heavy rifle fire was exceedingly destructive to the southeast angle and bomb-proof, scattering the covering of sand and blocking up the passageways. The engineer officer, Captain T. B. Lee, was powerless to arrest the destruction or repair the damages. Early in the afternoon of the second day of the bombardment the chief engineer, Colonel D. B. Harris, made his way through the terrific fire to Wagner to inspect the work and directed some alterations and repairs, leaving Captain F. D. Lee to relieve Captain T. B. Lee. But so destructive was the fire that it was found impracticable to work under it. Heroic endurance was all that remained for the besieged.

Soon after dark the sappers had pushed beyond and to the right of the south front, following the direction of the east or sea front and crowning the crest of the counterscarp near the flank of that front, completely masking the guns of the fort. A row of long pikes, which were planted at the foot of the counterscarp as an obstacle to an assault, were removed by the sappers early in the night. The long and heavy bombardment had so torn and cut down both scarp and counterscarp as to render the mounting of the parapets by a storming party comparatively easy. The sappers by spade and shovel had facilitated the ascent and only the light of another day was awaited for making the final assault of the work.

General Gillmore gave minute orders for the assault to be made at nine o'clock the next morning, that being the time of low tide, when the beach could be used for the movements of troops. Brigadier General A. H. Terry was ordered to command the assault in person.

On the 4th General Beauregard had called about him his general officers and chief engineer in consultation to determine how much longer it would be advisable to hold Wagner. The questions presented for consideration were, How long could it be held with regard to the safety of the garrison? How long without regard to the safety of the garrison? How long with reasonable prospect of ultimately withdrawing the troops? How long after the fall of Wagner could Battery Gregg be held? Could the heavy guns (two in Wagner and three in Gregg) be withdrawn without endangering the safety of the works and garrison, and, lastly, could the offensive be taken with fair prospect of success by throwing three thousand men on the north end of Morris Island in the night, which, with the garrisons of Wagner and Gregg, would make an effective force of about four thousand men, with the certainty that no more reinforcements could be sent them until the next night and probably not then?

The result of the deliberations was that the heavy guns were necessary for the defense of the posts to the last extremity; that there were, besides, insurmountable obstacles in the way of removing them, and that they should be ultimately disabled and left when it became necessary, as it was evident it soon would be, to abandon the batteries, which, however, should be held as long as communication with them by rowboats by night could be maintained.

Colonel Keitt kept the general commanding fully informed of the progress of the enemy's sap and the destructive effects of the fire. During the 6th he wrote: "The enemy will to-night advance their parallel to the moat of this battery (Wagner). The garrison must be taken away immediately after dark, as it will be destroyed or captured. It is idle to deny that the heavy Parrott shells have breached the walls and are knocking away the bomb-proofs. Pray have boats immediately after dark at Cummings' Point to take away the men. I say, deliberately, that this must be done or the garrison will be sacrificed. I am sending the wounded and sick now to Cumming's Point, and will continue to do so, if possible, until all are gone. I have not in the garrison four hundred effective men, excluding artillery. The engineers agree in opinion with me, or rather shape my opinion."

And again later: "The enemy's sap has reached the moat and his bombardment has shattered large parts of the parapet. The retention of the post after to-night involves the sacrifice of the garrison. If the necessities of the service make this advisable the men will cheerfully make it, and I will cheerfully lead them. I prefer to assault the enemy to await the assault and I will at four o'clock in the morning assail his works."

General Beauregard, accepting the situation, gave

minute instructions for the evacuation of Morris
Island.   Between 4 and 5 P. M. General Ripley
signaled the information to Colonel Keitt, and at
dark Captain McCabe, of General Ripley's staff,
delivered to the Colonel the General's instructions
for the evacuation.

On the morning of the 6th there were about nine
hundred Confederates on the island, only about two-
thirds of them effective, the others being wounded
or sick.   There were about nine thousand Union
soldiers on the island exclusive of the sick, and
the most advanced of them were abreast of Wagner, only across the street, as it were, from the
Confederates.   The space—about three-quarters of
a mile—between Wagner and Cumming's Point
where the garrison was to embark was swept by
the fire of the monitors, and there were armed
guard boats on the other side, in Vincent's Creek, to
give warning of any attempt to escape.

Anticipating pursuit, Lieutenant Robert M.
Stiles, engineering officer at Gregg, had constructed
after dark a rifle-pit across the island at a narrow
point a quarter of a mile in front of Gregg, from
which to cover the embarkation.   Two Confederate
ironclads, the *Charleston* and *Palmetto State,* under
Captain John R. Tucker, had taken position near
Fort Sumter, their guns bearing on Cumming's Point
and to the eastward of it, and the land batteries were
in readiness to sweep the water face of Battery
Gregg. Transport steamers were as near Cumming's Point as prudence would permit, to receive

the men from the small boats in which they were to leave the island.

During the two days' bombardment the sick and wounded had been sent to Cumming's Point as promptly as transportation between that point and Wagner could be provided, and they were first cared for and left the island in the first boats. Immediately after dark the movement from Wagner commenced; four companies (one hundred men) of the Twenty-fifth South Carolina Regiment, and a field piece taken from Wagner, moved first and embarked. Half an hour later Captain W. P. Crawford, with the Twenty-eighth Georgia Regiment and a howitzer, moved out, occupied the rifle-pits in front of Gregg and embarked by company as transportation could be in readiness. Major James Gardner, with the Twenty-seventh Georgia, succeeded the Twenty-eighth Georgia in the rifle-pits, and in turn was followed by the remainder of the Twenty-fifth South Carolina, Lieutenant Colonel J. G. Pressly commanding, and artillery.

The movement was made quietly and in admirable order, the majority of the men being under the impression that they were about to be relieved as usual, having served their tour of duty in Wagner. At eleven o'clock Colonel Keitt proceeded to Cumming's Point, leaving Captain Thomas A. Huguenin in Wagner commanding the rear guard, consisting of a few gunners and twenty-five men of the First and ten of the Twenty-fifth South Carolina, under Lieutenants F. B. Brown and B. M. Taft. As soon as the infantry had left Cumming's Point Captain H. R. Lesesne, who had for a long time commanded Battery Gregg, and Captain Kanapaux, commanding the three remaining howitzers, which he had just brought up from Wagner, spiked their guns and embarked their men.

Left in Wagner with about thirty-five men, Captain Huguenin kept up a slow fire, chiefly of sharpshooters, with an occasional mortar fire to deceive, if possible, his enemy as to his real purpose, and was busy with his final preparations. About midnight the rear guard was sent off, leaving Captain Huguenin, with Captain C. C. Pinckney and Lieutenant Mazyek, of the Ordnance; Lieutenant James A. Ross, of the Twenty-fifth South Carolina Volunteers, and Ordnance Sergeant Leath in Wagner to spike guns, destroy such property as they could, and lay the train to burst the only useful ten-inch gun in the work and to blow up the magazine.

In the meantime the Federal guard boats in Vincent Creek had discovered the passage of boats carrying away troops and opened fire upon them. Colonel Keitt dispatched a messenger to Captain Huguenin to say that boats were in readiness and that he must at once abandon the battery, which he did, reaching Cumming's Point about half-past one o'clock, under a rapid fire from the Union guard barges.

The safety fuse for blowing up the magazine of Battery Gregg was laid by the commissary of the post, Captain Holcumb, and was burning brightly when the last officer stepped into the boat, but from

some cause, probably defective fuse, neither magazine was blown up.

The steam transportation was under the management of Major Matt. A. Pringle, the embarkation
of the troops was superintended by Colonel Daut-
zler, Twentieth South Carolina Infantry, and the
small boats employed in moving the troops were
under the control of Captain W. H. Webb, of the
ironclad *Palmetto State.* The whole was conducted
systematically and with great success, only two
boats' crews of nineteen men and twenty-seven
soldiers falling into the hands of the enemy. Under
the circumstances of difficulty and peril which attended the movement in the face of an overwhelming
numerical force, it was marked by a degree of coolness and discipline worthy of the best tried veterans.

The different organizations in the military district
served there by turn, and were commanded succes-
sively by Brigadier Generals Taliaferro, Johnson
Hagood, A. H. Colquitt, and T. L. Clingman, and
Colonels George P. Harrison and Lawrence M.
Keitt. The Confederate loss on the island during
the whole fifty-eight days' operations was but 641
killed and wounded, and it is illustrative of the
sheltering capacity of sand that, deducting the loss
due to the descent on the island on July 10 and the
assaults of the 11th and 18th, the loss in killed and
wounded during the whole of the terrible bombardment was but 296 men. It is still more remarkable
that during the same period in the fire which demolished Sumter only 3 men were killed and 49
wounded. Before dawn on the 7th the Union

troops occupied both Wagner and Gregg, and were thus at last in possession of the little sand island of four hundred acres for which they had so perseveringly contended for nearly two months.

General Gillmore was rewarded by his government with a major general's commission, and there was naturally great exultation in the Union camp over the success of the operations on Morris Island. Salutes were fired and patriotic speeches delivered, but it was all too plain to intelligent men that they had at best achieved but a barren victory. The blow which had been aimed and delivered against Charleston with so much care had, as it were, glanced and exhausted its force on the end of a barren sandbank nearly four miles distant from the objective point of the campaign. From Cummings' Point the Union troops, still under Confederate fire, looked over a wide sheet of water bordered with heavy batteries and defended by torpedoes and other obstructions over which they must pass to reach Charleston.

CHAPTER XIV

Dahlgren demands surrender of Fort Sumter—Fort Moultrie engaged—Assault of Fort Sumter—Disastrous result—Army and navy mutually jealous—Obstacles in approach to Charleston—Can the harbor be entered?—Second bombardment of Fort Sumter—Sumter still resists—What now?—Operations against Charleston abandoned.

Having silenced Fort Sumter, reduced Battery Wagner, and occupied the whole of Morris Island, General Gillmore conceived that the land force had accomplished all that could be reasonably expected of it in the prosecution of the general plan of operations. To make the campaign a complete success it only remained, in his opinion, for the naval force to perform its part,—namely, to remove, if necessary, any obstructions that might be in its way, proceed to within easy range of Charleston and compel its surrender. That he thought could and should have been done at any time from August 23, when Sumter was apparently demolished, to September 7, when Battery Wagner was evacuated by the Confederate force and the island occupied by the Union troops; and he was exceedingly impatient at what he regarded as the culpable delay of the Admiral.

Admiral Dahlgren, however, did not think the time had yet arrived for making the attempt to enter the harbor with his ironclads. The Union flag should float over Sumter before, in his opinion, he could, with due consideration for the safety of his monitors, venture to carry them into the inner harbor. Early on September 7, when he learned that the Confederate troops had evacuated Morris Island, he sent, under flag of truce, to Major Stephen Elliott, commanding Fort Sumter, a demand for the surrender of that fort. Major Elliott refused to surrender his post, and forwarded the demand to General Beauregard, who replied that the Admiral could have Fort Sumter only when he could take and hold it. Preparatory to enforcing his demand, the *New Ironsides* and five monitors steamed up, and at about 6 P. M. took position between Cumming's Point and Fort Moultrie and opened fire on that fort, throwing an occasional shot into Sumter. The Sullivan's Island batteries replied, and until after dark a fierce cannonade was maintained, the *Ironsides* continuing the fire until nine o'clock.

During the night one of the monitors, the *Weehawken*, ran aground on Morris Island beach within range of Fort Moultrie. When it was discovered the next morning, Colonel William Butler, commanding Moultrie, opened fire on it, which was promptly returned, both firing with accuracy and effect. About nine o'clock five other monitors and the *Ironsides* came up and, taking positions varying from nine hundred to fifteen hundred yards from Moultrie, opened fire, and a furious cannonade was maintained for about five hours, when the fleet withdrew, leaving the *Weehawken* aground, and one monitor badly crippled. Usually in affairs between

the forts and monitors the former had the advantage
of being able to fire more rapidly than the latter.
On this occasion a scant supply of ammunition in
the land batteries made their fire slower than that
of the ironclads.   Early in the action a shell from
the *Weehawken* struck the muzzle of a columbiad in
Moultrie, and, glancing and bursting among some
ammunition, caused an explosion which instantly
killed sixteen and wounded twelve men of Captain
R. P. Smith's company of the First South Carolina
Infantry (Third Artillery).   Captain B. S. Burnet's
company of the same regiment was quickly brought
up from Battery Beauregard to supply the place of
Captain Smith's.   The fire had been mainly directed
against Moultrie, in which, in addition to the loss by
the explosion, three men were killed and two officers
(Captain G. A. Wardlaw and Lieutenant D. B. De-
Saussure) and fourteen men were wounded.   Lieutenant Edward W. Macbeth was wounded in Battery Beauregard and one officer and one man in Battery Bee.

While the affair between the ironclads and forts
was in progress, both the Admiral and General were
preparing to carry Fort Sumter by assault. Strangely
enough, both commanders were without concert preparing to assault the same work on the same night.
Whatever cordiality of feeling there may have been
between them seems to have ceased.   Each was confident of his ability to seize the work without the
aid of the other, and each ambitious of the honor of
capturing the fort which had so long resisted and
defied them.   Needing some additional boats for the

expedition, the Admiral sent to borrow them from the General. The latter replied that he could not spare them because he proposed to storm Sumter himself that night. Learning the General's intention, the Admiral seems to have desired co-operation, but declined the former's suggestion that the army officer commanding his storming party should also control the naval party. Each therefore proceeded independently of the other, the only agreement between them being that, to prevent accident of collision, of the two storming parties the first which entered the fort should display a red light from the battered walls.

The naval storming party consisted of 450 picked men, sailors and marines. Captain Thomas H. Stephens was selected to command it. The several divisions of boats were commanded by Lieutenants E. P. Williams, G. C. Raney, S. W. Preston, F. J. Higginson, T. M. Bunce, E. T. Brewer, and Ensigns James, Wallace, Porter, and Crane of the navy, and Captain C. G. McCawley, First Lieutenants Charles H. Bradford and John C. Harris, and Second Lieutenants R. L. Meade, Lyman P. Wallace, and L. E. Fagan, of the Marine Corps. Lieutenant Morean Forest was adjutant of the expedition.

The party assembled at the flagship *Philadelphia*, and left it in tow of the steam tug *Daffodil* about ten o'clock at night. When within about eight hundred yards of Sumter the tug stopped, the final instructions were given to the officers commanding the different divisions, the boats were cast off and pulled toward Sumter.

Lieutenant Higginson had been ordered to pull up to the northwestern front, for the purpose of drawing the attention of the garrison from the real point of attack. The remaining divisions were ordered to close up and await orders to advance upon the south front, where it was intended to make the assault. Captain Stephens' purpose for delaying the advance of the main body was to profit by all the advantage he hoped to derive from Lieutenant Higginson's diversion. The latter's movement, however, seems to have been mistaken by some of the boat commanders, for a general advance, "and, in that spirit of gallantry and emulation which characterize the service," says Captain Stephens, "they pulled for the fort." It was too late to stop the movement, and Stephens gave the signal for all to advance.

The demand for the surrender of Sumter had given significant warning that an assault was impending. Two Confederate ironclads were in position to sweep with their fire the exposed faces of Sumter. Forts Moultrie and Johnson were in readiness on a signal from Sumter to open fire.

Major Stephen Elliott, Jr., commanded the fort, which was garrisoned by the First South Carolina Battalion of Infantry, 205 men, under Major Julius A. Blake. A boat attack had been expected for several nights past, and one-third of the garrison was kept constantly under arms on the parapet, the remainder close at hand.

At one o'clock Major Elliott saw the fleet of barges approaching from the east. He immediately ordered up three companies, and reserved his fire until the boats had deployed and the men began to land, then opened fire. The outer boats returned the fire rapidly for a few minutes. The crews of those that had effected a landing rushed to the south wall, where they expected to find a practicable ramp formed by the débris of the wall, up which they might charge into the fort. They found indeed a ramp, but at the top of it a wall from fifteen to twenty feet high, and the storming party was not provided with scaling ladders. Unable to get in or away, they sought shelter under the projecting masses of the wall. Immediately on the signal of fire from Sumter, the ironclad *Chicora,* lying a short distance to the north, the Sullivan's Island batteries to the northeast, and Fort Johnson to the westward opened and encircled Sumter with their fire, effectually assisting to prevent the more distant boats from coming up. Some that had come nearest were disabled by hand grenades and masses of loose masonry hurled from the parapet. The men who had landed and sought shelter from fire under projecting masses of masonry were dislodged by hand grenades and fire balls. Cut off from reinforcements and escape, they called for quarter, and were ordered to make their way, by detachments, to the gorge of the fort, where they were taken within.

The boats which had, on a signal from Captain Stephens, not landed, turned and fled. "All who had landed," says Captain Stephens, "were killed or taken prisoners, and serious casualties occurred in the boats nearest the fort." Only eleven officers and 116 men had landed, of whom 6 were killed, 15 wounded, and 106 made prisoners. Five barges and as many colors were also captured. The affair ended in complete failure in about twenty minutes. Admiral Dahlgren, who was on a monitor about a quarter of a mile off, says: "Moultrie fired like a devil, the shells breaking around me and screaming in chorus. It did not look like a vigorous assault. Some of the boats' crews jumped overboard at the first fire, and I fell in with two boats a mile from Sumter. I came away without being able to see how the matter ended, and after a weary pull got on board the *Lodona*." He adds later in his journal: "Thus this attack on a fort which General Gillmore assumes he had demolished, necessarily failed."

General Gillmore's storming party consisted of six or seven hundred infantry. It was delayed somewhat by the state of the tide, but presently proceeded in barges, toward Sumter. When the firing of the naval party commenced, the barges halted, and when it was apparent that the naval attack had failed, they pulled back to Morris Island. Why the failure of the naval assaulting party should have induced the larger land force to abandon the assault which it had started, it is not easy to conceive. It would seem that the chances of success would have been enhanced if the two parties had assaulted simultaneously. And if made separately, the troops had a better prospect of success than the naval party, because the latter attempted the assault on a front where the breach was not practicable, whereas on the gorge front which troops would have assaulted there was and had been for some weeks a practicable breach.

"The result," says General Gordon, "did not dissipate the growing feeling of ill humor that had been for some time manifest between the land and naval forces. With no single head to devise and execute operations looking to the same end, there must needs be clashing and inefficiency and bad blood. In the meantime Sumter grew daily in strength."

For several weeks after gaining possession of Morris Island the Federal force was diligently at work altering and enlarging Batteries Wagner and Gregg to adapt them to the changed purposes for which they were designed, and in constructing new and formidable batteries between the two. A rather slow fire was maintained on the working parties by the batteries on James' and Sullivan's islands, enough to retard but not to prevent the construction of the work. If it had been possible under the most favorable circumstances, with the Confederate guns in position at so great a distance, to have prevented the construction of the Federal works, there was not ammunition enough in the Confederate batteries to have maintained an effective fire; nor was it practicable to procure a sufficient supply. Twenty tons of shot and shell per day would not have sufficed, and that could not be supplied. Late in September a slow fire was maintained from day to day on Sumter, enough as it was supposed, but erroneously, to prevent repairs and the remounting of guns.

The most favorable time for the ironclad fleet to attempt to force an entrance into the inner harbor was passing rapidly away; for while the Federals were busily at work on Morris Island the Confederates were not idle. They were strengthening the inner line of defensive works, arming them with guns taken from Sumter, and five or six were remounted in Sumter itself. Still the ironclad fleet made no attempt to enter, and to General Gillmore it seemed that the fruits of his success on Morris Island were passing away in consequence of the Admiral's delay. Newspaper correspondents near the General's headquarters sent to New York papers the most glowing accounts of the achievements of the army, giving little notice and no commendation to the part performed by the navy. On the contrary, the general tenor of the letters from the special correspondents at the seat of war in the Department of the South produced the impression that the delay of the naval commander alone prevented the complete fruition of all the hopes and expectations based on the campaign for the capture of Charleston.

Admiral Dahlgren was keenly alive to the delicacy and responsibility of his high position in the government service. He knew and shared the intensely hostile feeling pervading the North which demanded the reduction and occupation of Charleston, which was looked upon as the hotbed of secession and the initial point of the war. At the same time he fully appreciated the injury that would result to the cause he served with great zeal if any serious disaster should befall the ironclad fleet he com-

manded and which he deemed essential to the maintenance of the blockade of the port, a measure he
regarded as even more important than the occupation of the city itself.

One of his officers, Captain Daniel Ammen, reconnoitered and examined the obstructions stretching
from near Sumter across toward the northwestern
extremity of Sullivan's Island, and reported that
they could be removed, and that he, with volunteers
from the fleet, would make the attempt to remove
them. The Admiral seems to have entertained the
offer and given it serious thought. It is a significant
manifestation of the estimate he placed on the zeal
for the naval service of the men under his command,
that he suggested as a suitable and tempting reward
for gallant service to announce that those who sur-
vived the attempt should be honorably discharged
from the service. But the attempt was not made.
It was recognized that within the harbor were more
formidable obstacles to encounter than the rope and
timber and torpedo obstructions at its entrance.

Before leaving Washington to enter on the campaign, General Gillmore had expressed to the Secretary of the Navy his conviction that when he had
gained possession of Morris Island and had demolished Fort Sumter he could, with batteries erected
on Cumming's Point, silence the batteries on Sullivan's Island, thus completely opening the gate to
Charleston. His experience before Wagner had
long since demonstrated the utter hopelessness of
attempting to silence the Sullivan's Island batteries,

a mile and a half distant, across the channel. Those batteries were still intact.

The Admiral perhaps had that fact in mind when at this time he addressed a formal letter to General Gillmore, reminding him that the obstacles which barred the entrance to Charleston harbor had not yet been removed or destroyed. Sumter he regarded as still a serious obstacle in itself, and as guarding other obstructions. "The only fort you have attempted—Sumter—you have not reduced," and he asked that it be occupied by the Union troops. The General replied sharply, that from the concurrent testimony of the Confederates themselves, and the Admiral's own admission, Sumter was no longer regarded as capable of any harm to anyone. If, however, the Admiral thought, after only one abortive attempt on the part of the navy to capture the fort, that the few infantry soldiers who held it could offer any serious impediment to the removal of the obstructions between the fort and Sullivan's Island, he, the General, would remove them with his own troops. The Admiral replied, if the obstructions were to be removed, it was properly his province to remove them, and he did not need the services of the troops for that purpose. All he desired was that the Union troops should occupy the fort.

If the removal of the obstructions was regarded as an important preliminary to the entrance of the fleet, it was surely an excess of punctilio to stand on the order of their removal, whether by the land or naval force.

But in truth the obstructions were by no means so formidable as was supposed. There was no doubt risk to be encountered from submerged torpedoes, as was subsequently discovered by the explosion of one under the monitor *Patapsco* while covering an attempt to remove obstructions, instantly sinking the monitor and more than half of her crew, and like experiences elsewhere. But risks are inevitable, and these were such as the officers and men of the navy expected and were perfectly ready to encounter for the accomplishment of commensurate results. The difficulty was not so much to get *into,* as to get *out* of the inner harbor; and it was a question for grave consideration whether the results which might reasonably be expected to follow a successful entrance into the inner harbor would be at all commensurate with the risk to the ironclads. A glance at the map of the harbor will show that, leaving out of consideration Sumter and the formidable batteries on Sullivan's Island, there were seventeen batteries mounting fifty-eight guns covering the waters of the inner harbor. Long experience in the bombardment of Wagner and Moultrie had most clearly demonstrated that the combined land and naval batteries, throwing a weight of metal such as had never before been thrown on any work, could not permanently silence these land forts, or silence them any longer than they were immediately under fire. It would have been idle to suppose that the naval batteries alone could accomplish on the works within the harbor what the combined land and naval batteries had failed, under much more favorable circumstances, to effect on those without. There were, besides, two new and formidable Confederate ironclads within the harbor, which would have played a conspicuous part in any engagement in those waters. "The truth is," says Admiral Dahlgren, "that the entrance of ironclads could only make sure of the destruction of the city,—and not this without undue risk, if these were only monitors. The act itself could not be objected to by the Rebels, for it was understood to be their intent to destroy the place themselves rather than that we should occupy it. If so, it was quite as logical that we should destroy it rather than they should occupy it."

All arguments in favor of the entrance of the ironclads proceeded on the assumption that they were in good condition for action, which was far from being the case. They had all been under steam for six or seven months; their bottoms were so foul as materially to impair their speed; they had been repeatedly in action and were much damaged by the battering they had received, and two of the twenty-six guns they carried had been disabled and needed repairs before going again into action.

But public sentiment in the North clamored for the reduction of Charleston, and the "special correspondents at the seat of war" continued to lay the blame of the failure to accomplish that so eagerly desired consummation, to the navy.

At the instance of the Secretary of the Navy, Admiral Dahlgren, on October 24 convened a council of the ironclad captains, and in a session of six hours' duration the whole subject was discussed fully and without restraint. It was decided by a vote of six to four, the senior officers being in the majority, that an attempt to enter the harbor and proceed to the city would be attended with extreme risk without adequate results. To the question, Should the *Ironsides* enter with the monitors? there was no decision, —four for, four against, and two undecided; there was but one dissenting voice to the question, Would it be advisable to co-operate with the army in an attack on Sullivan's Island? and to the question, Can Forts Johnson and Moultrie be reduced by the present force of ironclads, unsupported by the army? the answer was unanimously *No*. The matter was briefly and forcibly stated by Commodore Rodgers in reply to an inquiry by a committee of the United States Senate, as follows:

"Ordinarily and popularly, to take a place means to take its defenses. General Gillmore was forty-eight[2] days on Morris Island, acting against Fort Wagner, with some ten or twelve thousand men against a garrison of about 1500 men or less, assisted by the monitors and by artillery which excited the wonder of Europe. After forty-eight days he took the place, not by his artillery nor by monitors, but by making military approaches and threatening to cut off their means of escape and take the place by assault; and when he took it, it was not so greatly damaged as to be untenable. Now, if General Gillmore, on the same island, assisted by his artillery and the whole force of the monitors, in forty-eight

[2] He was so engaged from July 10 to September 7.

days could not capture Fort Wagner alone by them, it is perfectly certain that the monitors alone never can take the much stronger defenses which line James Island and Sullivan's Island. In going up to Charleston, therefore, he would have to run by the defenses, and leave the harbor, so far as they constitute the command of it, in the power of the enemy; and when he got up to the city he could not spare a single man from his monitors, even if they should consent to receive him; and if he burned the town he would burn it over the heads of non-combatant women and children, while the men who defend it are away in the forts. I should be reluctant to burn a house over a woman's and child's head because her husband defied me. Dahlgren, if he burns Charleston, will be called a savage by all Europe, and after the heat of combat is over he will be called a savage by our own people. But there are obstructions in the way which render it doubtful whether he can get there. And if he goes up under the guns of those fortifications, sticks upon the obstructions, and is finally driven off by any cause, leaving one or two of his monitors there within their power, they will get them off, repair them, and send them out to what part of the coast they please and give a new character to the war. The wooden blockade will be mainly at an end, unlimited cotton going out and unlimited supplies coming in. I see no good to compensate for that risk, except it be in satisfying the national mind that retributive justice has been done against the city of Charleston, the nursery of the Rebellion. He might possibly go up there and burn the town, in which there are no combatants, and a place which, in a purely military point of view, as far as I know, possesses no value. To do that he risks losing vessels upon the obstructions, and if they should be so lost, and fall into the enemy's hands, a new phase will be given to the war. In a word, I do not think the game is worth the candle. Whether these reasons operate with him, I do not know; they would with me."

Admiral Dahlgren decided to make no attempt to enter the inner harbor until the monitors should be repaired, cleaned, and put in fighting trim, which would not be sooner than about the middle of November. He was, however, ready to co-operate with the land force in any operation it might undertake against Sullivan's Island or elsewhere. But General Gillmore, believing that he had accomplished his part of the general plan, was not disposed to enter on any new operations without reinforcements. His batteries at and near Cumming's Point being ready for action on October 26, he commenced what he calls the second bombardment of Sumter, in which the ironclads as usual bore a conspicuous part, their 11- and 15-inch guns being especially effective. This bombardment was maintained with great violence for about ten days, until many of the guns in the land batteries were worn out. The second bombardment had resulted in rendering the southeast face a more complete ruin than the gorge wall, and other faces were greatly shaken. What further to do to bring the compaign to a successful end was a most perplexing problem. Various projects were suggested and discussed in frequent conferences between the commanders of the land and naval forces. One was to attempt to capture Fort Johnson, but General Gillmore was unwilling to attempt to hold the ground west of Johnson or co-operate with the navy within the harbor, without an addition to his force of 15,000 men, and that he could not get. Another plan was to operate against Sullivan's Island by way of Bull's Bay. Since it seemed that Charleston could not then be taken, it was suggested that the combined force be turned upon Savannah and capture that city, and this project was discussed until it became known in Savannah, when preparations were in progress to meet it. Pending the consideration of these projects it was deemed advisable to divert public attention and let it be understood that further operations against Charleston were abandoned. General Gillmore undertook to have that report spread abroad by the special newspaper correspondents.

Meanwhile no explicit instructions came from Washington, and it was understood that the Secretary of War and the General-in-Chief of the army were averse to any further active operations at that time by the army against Charleston, the occupation of which they would have regarded as an "elephant on their hands."

Indeed, the purpose of the Administration in Washington in regard to Charleston is shrouded in some doubt, not withstanding the efforts made to capture that city.

In a letter from Colonel A. B. Ely, who had been

General Benham's chief of staff, to Major General G. W. Cullum, he says, referring to the failure of the assault on Secessionville June 16, 1862: "I could give you the reason of the want of success, but I need not now disparage anybody in that regard, nor is it needful that I should speak of the weak and wicked considerations which interfered to prevent any further action of General Benham in that direction, *particularly when I was assured by the President himself that he did not want we should take Charleston.*"[3]

Eighteen months after the assault on Secessionville, in December, 1863, General Gillmore, in conference with Admiral Dahlgren in regard to their future operations, said that the War Department had *"never entertained an idea beyond the occupation of the exterior islands."*

The exterior islands—Morris and Folly—were securely held, and a slow fire was maintained on the city and Forts Sumter and Moultrie; but whatever may have been the wishes of the Administration, General Gillmore's campaign of four months' duration virtually ended with the second bombardment of Fort Sumter.

[3]The letter is dated Boston, Mass., June 12, 1867.

Printed in July 2019
by Rotomail Italia S.p.A., Vignate (MI) - Italy